These Are My People

by Mildred T. Howard

for grade three

Designed for use with READING *for Christian Schools*® *3* and for the reading enjoyment of children of comparable ages

Bob Jones University Press, Greenville, South Carolina 29614

Illustrated by Roger Bruckner
Del Thompson

Cover illustration by Roger Bruckner

These Are My People

©1984 by Bob Jones University Press
Greenville, South Carolina 29614

Acknowledgments

Houghton Mifflin Company: Dictionary material based on the lexical
database of the *Children's Dictionary*, copyright ©1981 Houghton
Mifflin Company. No part of this book may be reproduced or
transmitted in any form or by any means, electronic or mechanical,
including photocopying and recording, or by any information stor-
age or retrieval system, except as may be expressly permitted by
the 1976 Copyright Act or with prior written permission from both
Houghton Mifflin Company and the Bob Jones University Press.

Dover Publications, Inc.: Chinese cut-paper designs from *Chinese Cut-
Paper Designs*, edited by Theodore Menten, copyright ©1975 by Dover
Publications, Inc.

20   19   18   17

Contents

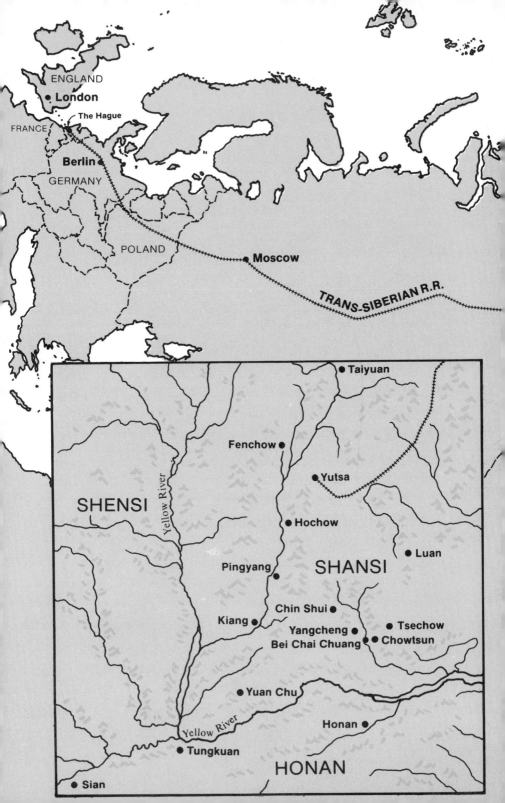

ENGLAND
London
The Hague
FRANCE
Berlin
GERMANY
POLAND
Moscow
TRANS-SIBERIAN R.R.

Taiyuan
Fenchow
Yutsa
SHENSI
Yellow River
Hochow
Luan
Pingyang
SHANSI
Chin Shui
Kiang
Tsechow
Yangcheng
Bei Chai Chuang
Chowtsun
Yuan Chu
Honan
Yellow River
Tungkuan
HONAN
Sian

Lord, Use Me!　　1

Gladys Aylward trudged wearily along a tree-lined street in North London, England. A cold wind shook the bare, dark branches of the trees and spattered drops of icy water down on her head. Shivering, she shifted the traveling bag to her other hand and turned up the collar of her coat.

Lamplight from the windows of the houses along Cheddington Road spilled pools of warmth into the blue twilight. At one of the houses Gladys stopped and pushed open a gate. She walked slowly up the path to the house. Opening the door quietly, she went in. From the kitchen came the sound of rattling dishes and merry laughter. Gladys put her bag down on the floor and went to the kitchen door. For a moment she stood without speaking, watching the three people in the room. Then, sensing a presence, they looked up.

"Gladys!"

"You're home!"

Gladys stepped into the warmth of the kitchen, arms outstretched. Mrs. Aylward was the first to reach her. She gave Gladys a quick hug, then released her to look at her face.

"Whatever is wrong, Gladys?" she asked. "Why are you home?"

"I didn't think you had a holiday until next month," Mr. Aylward said, half out of his chair, "but we're glad you could . . ."

"Gladys, welcome home!" Mr. Aylward's next words were drowned out by a happy greeting from Vi, Gladys's sister.

"Sit down, sit down," Mr. Aylward said, pulling out a chair. "You look tired."

When Gladys had removed her coat, Mrs. Aylward took one look and hurried to put the stew back on the stove. Gladys had always been thin for her five-foot height, and lately she had been studying too hard to stop and eat much. Her usually sparkling brown eyes now looked too big for her thin, pale face. Even with her long dark hair pulled back and coiled into a bun, she still looked younger than her twenty-eight years.

"Now," Mrs. Aylward said firmly, returning to sit at the table with the others, "what has happened? What's wrong?"

Gladys gave them a tired smile. "The principal of the China Mission Board recommended that I not return for another school term. I won't get to go to China."

"But why?"

"What happened?"

"You know that I have always had trouble studying," Gladys explained, "but I thought that if I really tried hard I could do better. I listened, I took notes, and I even recopied the notes of other students. The other students studied with me. But when it came to test time, facts and numbers just seemed to run out of my mind."

"Oh, Gladys," Vi said sadly. "I wish I could have helped."

Gladys gave her sister a hug. "It wouldn't have done any good, Vi. Everyone helped as much as they could. The problem is with me."

"You tried everything possible?" Mr. Aylward asked.

"Everything."

"Then you won't be studying to be a missionary at all," Mrs. Aylward said slowly.

"No, Mum." Gladys shook her head. "Even if I could go another year at the Mission School it would be too late to send me to China. I'm twenty-eight years old now. I would be almost thirty before I finished the courses."

"What's wrong with that?" Vi asked. "You're not old!"

"No, but younger people have an easier time

learning the language and the new customs. Chinese is a very difficult language. The principal says it takes months, even years of study to master it." Gladys sighed. "And that's for people who learn a lot faster than I do."

"You do other things well," Mrs. Aylward said gently. "You are a good worker, you witness to others, and you love the Lord."

Mr. Aylward leaned forward. "Don't be discouraged, Gladys. Mum is right. You do many things that are needed right here as well as in China. Maybe the Lord wants to use you here."

"That's what the principal said," Gladys replied quietly. "I really thought the Lord wanted me to go to China—I really did. But perhaps you are right, and I was wrong."

"So what will you do now?" Mrs. Aylward asked.

"I'll get a job as a parlour maid again," Gladys replied. "But first I'm going to Bristol. The principal asked me to help two missionaries that have recently returned from China. At least I'll learn more about China from them. After that I'll look for a job."

"Can you stay with us for a few days before you go to Bristol?" Vi pleaded.

Gladys smiled. "Yes, if it's all right with Mum and Dad."

"We're always happy when you visit, Gladys." Mr. Aylward looked affectionately at his older daughter. "It'll give Mum time to put some meat on your bones."

"Of course you can stay." Mrs. Aylward got up quickly. "Vi, the stew is bubbling. Bring a bowl for Gladys while I put some fresh sheets on her bed."

The next few days were happy ones for Gladys. She laughed at Dad's jokes, worked in the kitchen with Mum, went on walks with Vi, and enjoyed every minute of her time with her family.

One day Gladys sat down at the old organ in the parlour and pumped the pedals. Vi came to sit on the bench with her.

"He died that we might be forgiven, He died to make us good, that we might go at last to Heaven, saved by His precious blood," they sang.

Mrs. Aylward came to the parlour door to listen. When Gladys stopped playing, her mother said, "Remember when the bombers flew over the house during World War I? You and Vi would bring all the neighborhood children into the parlour. Then you would play the organ and everyone would sing and sing as if singing would drive the planes away!"

Gladys laughed, her warm brown eyes twinkling. "It may not have driven the planes away, but it did help us not to be afraid."

Her mother laughed. "Singing does help, doesn't it? Remember when . . ."

"Remember how . . ."

"Remember what . . ."

They told tale after tale of the growing-up days. Gladys and Vi had both been born in the house on Cheddington Road in Edmonton. Once it had been at the edge of open fields. Over the years the fields had been replaced by the red brick buildings of North London. The neighbors up and down the now crowded street were old friends. They, too, were happy to see Gladys again.

Many of the neighbors had been led to the Lord by Gladys. All of them knew of her testimony. After years of seeing her attend meetings, work with the youth groups, and become stronger in her faith day by day, few had been surprised when Gladys decided she wanted to be a missionary. Now they encouraged her, reminding her of the work she had done in her own neighborhood.

"Stay and work with the youth groups," one neighbor suggested. "The children love you, Gladys."

"And I like working with them," Gladys said. "I don't know. I thought I would get a job as parlour maid again, but perhaps I could do something for the Lord here in England."

"China is a long way away," the neighbor said, patting Gladys on the hand. "At least if you work in England, we'll get to see you sometimes."

Soon her few days of rest were over. Gladys went to stay with the missionaries at Bristol as she had planned. The two missionaries were as much a comfort to Gladys as she was to them. They told her thrilling tales of how God had helped them through difficulties. Gladys listened in amazement.

Gladys didn't look for a job as a parlour maid. She decided instead to work for the Lord. "Somewhere," Gladys thought, "God has a place for me. If it isn't China, then He will show me."

For many months Gladys tried to find out what it was God wanted her to do. She worked as a helper at a hostel for women. She worked with friends, trying to help the poor. Then she took a job as assistant matron in a hostel for women in Swansea.

Hard times had left many people without jobs. Gladys went from house to house, witnessing and trying to help in any other way she could. In the houses she learned not to flinch when rats ran through the hallways. She learned not to be shocked when she saw dozens of families crowded into one building, thankful for a roof over their heads. But she never learned to hide her distress when she saw ragged children shivering in the drafty, poorly heated rooms.

Gladys gave away every piece of clothing she could, and then wrote home for family and friends to send more.

"You're doing a good work there," Mum wrote. "That must be the place God has for you."

"Yes, this is a good work," Gladys wrote back. "But it just isn't where the Lord wants me to stay. Somehow, some way, I know God wants me in China."

Every month Gladys became more certain of God's call to China. Finally, she bought a train ticket back to Edmonton. "I'll be a parlour maid again," she said to herself. "I'll save every penny I can. And when I have enough money, I'll go to China!"

At home, Mr. Aylward listened as Gladys explained what she wanted to do. "You're planning to go on your own, not through a mission board?"

As Gladys nodded, Mrs. Aylward gasped.

"All on your own? Where will you stay? What will you do?"

"You're not a teacher or a nurse," Mr. Aylward said.

"No, I'm not." Gladys shook her head.

"Then what will you do in China?"

"Just tell them about Christ, as I do here. I guess I talk better than I do anything else." Gladys smiled a little.

"You've prayed about this, Gladys, really prayed?" her father asked.

When Gladys nodded, he said quietly, "Then somehow God will work it out, Gladys. We'll do everything we can to help you too."

Gladys stayed at her parents' house in Edmonton until she found a job at a house in London's Belgrave Square. The train fare to her new place of employment took almost all of the money she had saved. When Gladys arrived at the house she was taken to a small room. She looked around the room at the bare walls, the narrow bed, and the neat washstand with its white china jug and basin. Her courage deserted her, and she sat down on the bed in despair.

"Thirty years old and a maid again!" Gladys thought. "It won't work! I'll be stuck here forever. I'll never make enough to get to China!"

Her Bible lay before her on the table by the bed. Taking out the few coppers she had, she placed them on top of the Bible. Then she clutched both money and Bible in her hands.

"Oh, God," she cried out loud. "Here's my Bible! Here's my money! Use me, Lord, use me!"

Through her tears she heard a voice calling her name. Quickly wiping her eyes, she went to the door.

"The mistress wants to see you," a maid said, looking curiously at Gladys's reddened eyes.

Gladys followed the maid down the stairs. By the time they reached the parlour the tears were gone, and Gladys was able to meet her mistress with her usual cheerful smile.

"Gladys," her employer said to the small woman standing in front of her, "I always allow my new employees traveling expense to my home. How much did it cost you to come from Edmonton to Belgrave Square?"

Her heart beating rapidly, Gladys told her employer the amount. In amazement Gladys watched as the coins were counted into her hand. When the interview was over, Gladys rushed back up the stairs. In her room she carefully placed on her Bible ten times the amount of money that was already there.

Joyfully she said, "If God can multiply like this, I'm going to China! I'm really going to China!"

Tickets to China   2

After a few weeks at work, Gladys went on her half day off to the Haymarket shopping area. She was looking for Mullers', the travel agency. When she found it, she stopped for a moment to look at the brightly colored travel posters in the window. Then she opened the door and went inside. An elderly booking clerk was working at the counter. Gladys stopped in front of him.

"How much is a ticket to China?" she asked.

The booking agent stopped shuffling papers and looked directly at Gladys. His gaze traveled over her worn coat and stopped at her face. Her dark eyes and warm smile made him forget the sarcastic remark that he had intended to make. Instead he asked, "Why China? China's a long way from home, young lady. How about Paris?"

Gladys laughed. "Paris is not for me. I have

missionary work to do in China. How much will it cost to go there?"

The booking agent shook his head and told her the price.

Dismayed, Gladys clutched her thin purse. It would take forever to raise that much money!

"Isn't there a cheaper way?" she pleaded. "There must be!"

"Sure," the booking agent replied, pushing his cap back on his head. "It costs less than fifty pounds to cross Europe and Russia and go through Siberia . . . but you'll not be going that way."

"Why not?"

"Because there's a war going on between Russia and China. We're not sending passengers out on that line."

"But I want to get a ticket."

"It would take more than one ticket," the agent said wearily. "Now look, young lady. We like to deliver our passengers alive. There'll be no passengers from England on that line."

Gladys opened her purse, took out three pound notes, and put them on the counter. "Well, I'm paying on account. By the time I get the tickets paid for, the war will probably be over," she said cheerfully. "I'll be back next week with some more money."

The booking agent held up his hands. "All right, all right, if that's the way you want it."

From then on, Gladys began to work extra on her half days off. She helped at parties at other houses. She walked instead of taking the train or bus. Every penny she could spare, she saved. And every spare moment she had, she devoted to Bible study.

Finally, one night after a church meeting, someone told Gladys, "I know an elderly missionary in China. Her name is Mrs. Jeannie Lawson. She came home a few years ago to retire but couldn't adjust to London. She went back to China to spend her remaining years trying to reach the Chinese for Christ. She is praying for a young person to come out and help her."

"That's me!" Gladys said joyfully.

Gladys made plans to join Mrs. Lawson in China. All she had to do was get to Tientsin, where someone would meet her and take her to Mrs. Lawson. Now what free time she had was spent at home in Edmonton, preparing for the trip. At last the day came when Gladys plunked down the last shilling on the ticket counter.

"That's the last of it," Gladys said triumphantly. "What tickets do I get?"

The booking agent looked at her gloomily as he tore off the tickets. "Does your family know you're going to China? That war's still going on, you know."

Gladys thought with pleasure of the orange dress Mum had taken in for her, the cap-like hat Vi had made to keep her head warm, and all the other preparations that had made the house in Edmonton fairly buzz with excitement.

She gazed back at the agent, her eyes sparkling with excitement. "Oh yes, they know that God has called me to China," she replied happily.

The agent handed her the tickets and leaned closer. "Take care of yourself, little lady!"

"God will take care of me," Gladys replied with a cheery wave. "Good-bye!" she called, and she walked away, humming happily.

On the fifteenth of October, 1932, Gladys Aylward set off for China. She wore a blue reefer coat over the orange dress and carried two suitcases. One of the cases held clothes; the other held food. The rest of her baggage consisted of a roll of bedding, a brown paper bag containing a spirit stove, and a kettle and saucepan tied together with string.

One of her friends had made a rug from an old fur coat. "This is for you," she said as she handed it to Gladys. "I wanted to know that you'd be warm, even going through Russia!"

A group of Gladys's friends had come to see her off. Mum and Vi were there, but Dad left early because he couldn't bear to see Gladys leave. The Cross Channel train was drawn up at Liverpool Station. Porters rushed by, pushing trunks and suitcases along the crowded platform. Elegant passengers swept into the first-class compartments, while shabbier ones carried their own parcels and boxes into third-class compartments. Little groups gathered and broke apart and gathered again, laughing and crying. The whistle blew, the stragglers ran, and the guard waved his flag.

"Good-bye!"

"God bless you!"

"Good-bye!"

Gladys settled herself in a compartment and arranged her belongings as neatly as possible. She took out the note pad and pen she had brought to record her thoughts and placed it on the seat. Then she began to talk to her traveling companions. Her open cheerfulness made friends quickly as the train rattled toward the coast.

At Hull, Gladys left the train and boarded a boat for the short passage across the English Channel. She stepped ashore at The Hague. She was farther away from home than she had ever been in her life.

At The Hague, she got on the continental train. Gladys sat comfortably in a corner seat, facing the engine, and watched Europe pass before her eyes. At mealtimes she helped herself from the suitcase filled with cans of corned beef, fish, baked beans, hard-boiled eggs, powdered coffee, beef tea, crackers, and rye crisps. She wrote letters and took daily walks through the train corridor for exercise.

As the train rumbled on through Germany, Gladys found it more difficult to find people who could speak English. Just before they reached Berlin, a girl in the next compartment overheard Gladys trying to communicate with a conductor. She came to Gladys's rescue. That night Gladys slept in the girl's home and was given a tour of Berlin. What a relief it was to be off the swaying train!

"Everything in Germany is neat and orderly,"

Gladys wrote in her note pad, "not a bit like England."

When she boarded a train for Moscow, her only companion was a Polish man. Communication now became a matter of sign language. "As far as officials are concerned," Gladys wrote, "I cannot understand them, so I just shake my head!"

As the train sped toward Russia, soldiers in polished boots and blue uniforms boarded the train. Gladys stared in amazement as they searched under the seats and behind the curtains. The procedure was repeated often, and she became used to it. Each time the soldiers came looking through her compartment, she gave thanks that England was a free country.

As the train slowed for towns, Gladys saw a sight that made her heart ache. Small children were working on the roads in the icy cold. "I can't believe Russia is happy," she wrote in her note pad. "The poor people look so miserable."

In Moscow Gladys was to change trains. She stood up and stretched to ease her cramped body. Then, carrying her baggage, she stepped onto the platform. She walked to the tap to fill her kettle with water. The buckets under the tap were full of ice, but the taps worked when Gladys turned them on. Humming to herself, she sat down and made tea on her spirit stove.

As she ate, the platform filled with soldiers. They walked up and down the snow-spattered platform, waiting for trains. Gladys watched them uneasily as they moved past her. These men were different from the others she had seen. They did not wear neat uniforms. Dirty and untidy, the soldiers carried bread tucked under their arms. From time to time they tore off chunks and stuffed the pieces into their mouths. The usual happy and sad tones of arriving and departing passengers were absent. Gladys shivered at the strange tenseness that gripped the station.

When her train arrived, Gladys climbed quickly aboard. She was so relieved to leave Moscow that sharing a compartment with three men did not bother her. Unafraid, Gladys calmly curled her hair, put on her sleeping cap, said her prayers, and went off to sleep wrapped in her warm fur rug.

Throughout the journey the men treated her with politeness. Although they could speak no English, they tried to take care of Gladys. They got off at the few snow-blanketed stations to make sure her kettle was kept full of water. Sometimes even the taps on the platforms were frozen, and Gladys had no hot coffee or tea on those days. More and more often, she found it necessary to walk briskly up and down to get warm. Then she wrapped herself in her rug again and slept.

The train chugged on over the vast, lonely steppes of Russia. For hours Gladys saw only an occasional wild animal from the train window.

At night the setting sun cast a red glow over the huge banks of black clouds and made the snow-covered land look like a golden sea.

In spite of the biting cold, the wild, beautiful landscape and the nearness of China gave Gladys such happiness that she began to sing, "I walk with the King, hallelujah!" Everyone in the carriage smiled.

That day a man who could speak some English boarded the train. The other passengers and Gladys put him to work as an interpreter. The other passengers wanted to know everything about Gladys, and her curiosity was as strong as theirs! Before the man left the train, however, he delivered a message to Gladys from the conductor.

"There are no trains running to Harbin because of the fighting," he said.

Gladys's cheerfulness disappeared at once. She couldn't eat supper. That night she sat up. "I am failing God," she thought. She reached for her Bible. As she opened it, a small piece of paper fell out. Picking it up, she read, "Be not afraid, remember the Lord." God had been taking care of her. How could she not trust Him now?

When the train stopped at Chita, all the passengers in Gladys's compartment got off. Gladys sat still, looking out the window. Besides the passengers who got off the train, only soldiers were on the platform. They filed noisily onto the train. No one came into Gladys's compartment.

Gladys hesitated. The train began to move.

Gladys got up and made her way through the next compartment. It was empty. Her heart pounding, she hurried through the aisles. The soldiers looked at her curiously but didn't speak. Except for the soldiers, Gladys was the only passenger on the train!

For four hours the train chugged through the darkness. Gladys sat alone in her compartment. At last the train ground to a stop. The soldiers leaped off and rushed out into the swirling snow. Gladys wiped off her window and tried to see outside. The train was still and strangely quiet. Then, suddenly, she heard the rattle of gunfire!

Her face pale, Gladys drew the rug over her shoulders and waited. No one entered the train. There was no sound other than the distant gunfire. Finally, Gladys got up and stepped down onto the platform. In a hut at the end of the platform she saw the gleam of a lantern. She walked slowly toward the hut. When she reached the door, she recognized the train crew. Using motions, she tried to talk to them.

Gladys pointed up the tracks and raised her hands questioningly. The men only shrugged. They pointed back down the track to Chita. At last Gladys understood that there would be no more trains. Even this train would not move until it was loaded with the wounded. Gladys was on the edge of a battlefield. Beyond the battlefield was Manchuria . . . the Chinese border.

Gladys strained to see into the darkness. "I'm so close," she thought, "so close!" Slowly she gathered her two suitcases, the bedding, and the packages. Pulling the rug around her shoulders, she stepped off the platform. A small, thin shadow against the darker night, Gladys began the long walk back down the railroad tracks to Chita.

Escape from Russia 3

Gladys plodded along slowly between the railroad tracks. On each side of the tracks huge, snow-burdened trees stretched toward the dark sky. Falling snow filled her footprints behind her as she walked.

"Over four hours by train," Gladys thought. "How long will it take me to walk back to Chita?"

Putting the thought of time from her mind, she walked on. The soft plopping sound made by snow falling from the tree branches sounded like footsteps. Gladys peered into the darkness but saw nothing. Then in the distance she heard a long howl. Frightened, she began to walk faster.

"This is silly," she said to herself. "God is here; I'm not alone."

She began to sing loudly. "Count your blessings, name them one by one . . ." she half shouted into the darkness. Then she stopped and laughed at herself. "I'm singing fear away again, as Mum would say." Comforted, she began to sing again quietly, "Count your blessings, see what God has done. . . ."

Every so often she stopped to adjust her bundles and hitch the fur rug back over her shoulders, and then she would start out again, still singing. Gradually the songs became whispers, and Gladys began to stumble.

"I've got to rest," she said aloud. "If the trains aren't running, this is as good a place as any."

Gladys put her suitcases down on the track and got out her spirit stove. From her dwindling supply of food she took out some stale crackers and a bit of tea. Sheltering the flame from the wind and snow, she lit her stove. As the water boiled in the kettle, she warmed her hands over the steam. Then she sat down on the tracks to eat. After the first mouthful, she began to laugh. "Here I am in the middle of nowhere," she said out loud, "having tea in a snowstorm!"

After eating, Gladys felt a little better, although she was still tired and sleepy. She put her suitcases off the track, making a barrier against the icy wind. Then she stacked her bundles on the other side of the suitcases. Wrapping herself in the fur rug, she crawled between the suitcases and the bundles. For a while she lay still, thanking God for His care. Then, as snow dusted the fur rug with white, Gladys closed her eyes and slept.

When she awoke it was morning. Gladys lifted one corner of the rug and peeped out. The snow had stopped. She pushed back the snow-covered rug and crawled out. Shaking off the rug, she wrapped it back around her. Then she picked up her belongings and began to walk again.

Snow lay in smooth banks on either side of the tracks. The snow that had drifted over the tracks crunched lightly under Gladys's feet as she walked. She walked quickly for a while, stopping often to rest. At noon she sat down and made hot tea and ate some crackers. Then she walked on. By mid-afternoon her steps had slowed. But not wanting to sleep on the tracks again, she struggled on. Night came, but she didn't stop. At last she saw lights sparkling in the distance.

It was late in the evening before Gladys stumbled onto the platform at Chita. Half frozen, she tried to get help, but the people didn't understand her. Finally she sat huddled on her packages, trying to keep them from being stolen out from under her. She was cold and hungry and frightened. Seeing that no help was coming, she thought, "If I make a commotion, they'll have to arrest me. Then I'll get help!"

Gladys sang "I'm a Child of the King" as loudly as she could, and then shouted verses one after the other. From time to time a soldier would come along and try to get her to move. Gladys just hung on to her suitcases and bundles and shook her head. At last an official appeared and took charge. Gladys meekly picked up her bundles and followed him.

He led her to a dirty room crowded with rough-looking men. Gladys took out her passport and showed it to the official. He immediately called a guard and had Gladys moved to another room.

For hours Gladys tried to explain that she was a missionary on her way to China.

"Missionary! Missionary!" she said over and over. "China!"

They understood China, but they were still puzzled. Gladys seemed to be going away from China, and she was walking!

The official pointed to her passport. Chita had already been stamped. Why, then, was she back in Chita?

At last Gladys made enough motions to convince the men that battle had stopped her. Then they puzzled at length over the word *missionary* and decided that it had something to do with machines.

"No, no!" Gladys shook her head. "Not machine, missionary!"

In despair Gladys pulled out her Bible and leafed through it, showing them picture after picture. "Missionary!" she exclaimed.

Finally they seemed satisfied. Gladys was given another visa. The official insisted on showing Gladys around Chita while she waited for another train. When the train arrived, Gladys was given directions that would take her around the fighting. With relief she boarded the train. She was on her way again.

But when she reached the next station, she found that the conductor's warning was right. No trains were going to Harbin. "Go to Vladivostok!" Gladys was told. The station was crowded with people. Tiny Gladys was pushed aside, and she missed the first train. When the next one entered the station, a wiser and more determined Gladys shoved her way aboard. She fell triumphantly into an empty seat. Pushing her hair back out of her eyes, she tucked her belongings under her feet. She smoothed as many of the wrinkles as she could out of her orange dress and settled down for a nap. Eventually Gladys reached Vladivostok, a port on the great Sea of Japan.

Again Gladys could not make herself understood. When an old man tried to steal her stove, she rushed back to her bundles. She spent another sleepless night on the train platform, guarding her possessions. The next morning she tried to talk to the officials again. After giving up on everything else, she pulled a picture of her brother from her purse. The officials looked at the well-dressed picture of a soldier and seemed impressed. Quickly they whisked Gladys off to a hotel. Dirty and worn down as the hotel was, she was thankful that she didn't have to spend another night out in the open. She stopped at the hotel desk to explain her situation. Another official looked at her passport.

"A missionary?" he asked, raising his eyebrows.

Gladys nodded thankfully, happy to meet someone who spoke English. The man looked her over carefully.

"You are small, but you look strong," he said thoughtfully. "Perhaps you have also worked on machines?"

Gladys's heart sank. "No, no. I am a missionary. I know nothing about machines."

"Russia has need of many young people to work machines," the official continued. "You wish to help others. Why not stay and help us?"

Gladys's eyes sparkled with determination. She shook her head. "God has sent me to China," she said firmly. "My work is there."

The official tapped her passport lightly. "We shall see," he said softly. As Gladys reached for the passport, he pulled it back. "I will keep this for the time being," he said.

Gladys was too tired to argue. She followed him to her room.

"See," he said, "a nice room and a bath."

"A bath!"

When she was finally alone, Gladys soaked in the tub. She wrote home, "Oh the joy to be clean! This is the first time I have bathed since I left home!"

The next morning the official was waiting for Gladys. He walked her to the door, smiling.

"Why not let me show you our city while you are waiting?"

The official spent several days showing Gladys around Vladivostok. While he pointed out buildings with pride, Gladys saw muddy, pot-holed roads. When he talked of the opera, she saw long lines of people waiting for food. As he showed her the boats in the busy harbor, Gladys saw soldiers with drawn bayonets guarding the docks.

The cold wind from the sea swept through the muddy streets. Even when she huddled in the doorways, Gladys could not escape its icy gusts.

"I want to go to China," she told the official. "Let me have my passport."

"Why not stay here?" he suggested. "We will take good care of you."

Gladys trembled. "I am going to China!"

The official only smiled. He took her back to the hotel. As Gladys walked down the hall, she passed a young girl. The girl reached out to touch Gladys's arm. Startled, Gladys stopped.

"Quick, did he take your passport?" the girl whispered.

"Yes," Gladys said, staring at the girl. "Why?"

"It will be changed to say that you are a machinist," was the quick reply. "We can't talk here. Wait for me in the alley."

Surprised and wondering, Gladys walked quickly out of the building. She looked carefully at the people walking down the street, but no one seemed to be paying any attention to her. Gladys shook her head impatiently.

"This is silly," she thought. "I'm acting just like a spy!"

Then, remembering the other time an official had thought she was a machinist, she decided to follow the girl's instructions.

At the dark alleyway, Gladys hesitated a moment. She took a last look around and darted into the shadows. She waited, shivering. The minutes ticked by slowly.

Gladys caught her breath as a dark form slipped into the alley. It moved nearer cautiously, and Gladys recognized the young girl.

"You must leave here," the girl whispered rapidly. "Tonight!"

"Why?"

"They will change your passport and send you to a work camp," the girl replied. "You must get away."

"But how can. . ."

"If you can get your passport, you can leave on a ship tonight. I know someone who will take you."

"I have no money," Gladys gasped.

"It does not matter," the girl answered. "He will take you anyway. A friend will knock on your door just after midnight. Go with him."

Stunned, Gladys nodded.

The girl turned to leave. "Wait here until I have gone. Don't forget to get your passport!"

Gladys was still trembling when she reached her room at the hotel. She knelt beside her bed and began to pray.

"I know the Lord has kept me safe this far, and He can help me now," she thought. "He will take care of me."

Still on her knees, she began to sing softly,

Sweet hour of prayer, sweet hour of prayer,
That calls me from a world of care,
And bids me at my Father's throne
Make all my wants and wishes known;

In seasons of distress and grief,
My soul has often found relief,

And oft escaped the tempter's snare,
By thy return, sweet hour of prayer.

When her passport was returned that afternoon, Gladys was no longer afraid. Leaning against her door, she opened the passport. The light from the dangling bulb showed her the change that had been made. Instead of missionary it now said machinist!

At midnight the knock on the door came softly. Gladys was ready. She opened the door quickly. The man waiting in the hall gave her a quick smile. Quietly Gladys followed him out of the hotel, down to the docks, and onto the Japanese boat. There he left her in the care of the captain. Under cover of night, Gladys left Russia.

West of the Mountains   4

When Gladys arrived in Japan, she was delighted with the people and the country. After the unhappiness of Russia, it was a relief to see smiling faces again. Japan was almost as cold as Russia, but the houses and brightly painted gates were hung with colorful flags and banners that rippled in the wind. "How pretty everything is!" Gladys exclaimed. She walked slowly down a street in Kobe, trying to look in every direction at once. As she stopped to admire a beautifully patterned gate, a Japanese rickshaw stopped beside her. Its driver called loudly to Gladys.

Laughing, Gladys pushed her suitcases and bundles into the seat and climbed in. The driver looked back at her and spoke rapidly. Gladys nodded, not knowing what he said. With a jerk, the rickshaw began to move. They wove in and

out of the crowds, through street after street. They passed shops full of people. Women wearing brightly colored kimonos hurried from shop to shop. Shopkeepers called to workers. Everyone seemed to be busy. While Gladys was looking at the shops, the rickshaw passed a sign that said "Kobe Baptist Mission."

Gladys gave a startled cry. The rickshaw driver stopped. With quick motions Gladys let him know that she wanted to go into the mission. Inside she found a missionary couple from England.

They were delighted to have a visitor from home. They took Gladys to their home to spend the night.

Gladys marveled at their clean home and its neatly pebbled courtyard. She was given her own room overlooking the courtyard. That night she bathed in a wooden tub and slept in a white bed with blue covers. Over her head hung a blue and white lantern.

Gladys wrote, "I thought I knew the value of prayer before but never as now. When everything seemed against me, He was there ready to help me over the difficult places. Now here I am safe and happy, just waiting to go on. I would willingly go through it all again for the joy of knowing my Saviour as I know Him now."

The next morning the missionaries took her to see the British consul. He agreed to get her remaining tickets exchanged for a boat ticket to China, and railway tickets in China. Gladys was soon on her way again, traveling by boat across the water to China.

When the boat docked, Gladys was finally looking at the shore of China. Triumphant praises rang in her mind as she stood in the land to which God had sent her. "It's taken almost a month of traveling," she said aloud, "but I'm here! I'm really here!"

"Or almost," she thought to herself. "On to Tientsin, then to Mrs. Lawson!" Then a thought clouded her happiness. "I'm over a week late.

What if my guide is no longer waiting?" she wondered. Then she dismissed the thought. "I'll trust God to take care of me."

When she reached Tientsin, she met Mr. Lu. The Chinese evangelist who worked with Mrs. Lawson was still waiting for her. The quiet man was dressed in a black Chinese robe and wore a fedora on his head. Gladys was delighted when she discovered that he spoke English. She bombarded him with questions as they boarded a train that would take them to Peking, and then on to Yutsa, where the railroad ended.

"What is Mrs. Lawson like? How many people are at the mission? What is the mission like?" Mr. Lu smiled and answered as many of her eager questions as he could. He helped her place her packages under the wooden seat and then sat down beside her. As the train chugged out of Tientsin, he pointed out a Mohammedan mosque. "There are ten mosques here," he said, to Gladys's surprise. "China is a land of many religions. Buddhism, Taoism, Islam, and Judaism are the most common. Few Chinese are Christians. The fields are truly white for harvest."

The train left the town and clattered through rolling farmlands. Gladys saw pigtailed farmers dressed in plain blue garments. A few drove two-wheeled carts pulled by small Mongolian ponies. Others pushed wheelbarrows piled high with bundles. Mud-walled farmhouses and villages were bordered by stubbled fields. At every station vendors ran along the train windows trying to sell their wares to the passengers. At the station in Peking an armful of lotus blossoms were thrust through Gladys's window.

"How beautiful!" Gladys sighed, touching the waxy flowers before returning them to the vendor. "No, no, I have no money," she said, shaking her head.

Soon the train left the lowlands and began to climb toward the snowcapped mountains. The hills were circled by terraced fields frosted with snow. Behind them lay a half circle of distant mountains. As the train continued to climb, the hills became more barren and stony. Mr. Lu pointed to holes in some of the hills. "Mines?" Gladys asked.

"No, although there are coal mines in Shansi province. These are cave dwellings—houses hollowed out of the ground."

"But I thought those were houses," Gladys said, pointing to a gray bricked wall.

"They are," Mr. Lu said. "Not everyone lives in caves, of course. There are palaces and mud-walled huts, temples and roadside inns."

At Yutsa the railway ended. Gladys followed Mr. Lu to a building near the station. "We must take the bus to Tsechow," he explained. "We will meet Mrs. Lawson there."

They boarded an old bus crowded with Chinese. The passengers moved aside to allow room for Gladys and Mr. Lu. He motioned Gladys to a seat beside a window. Gladys was thankful for both the view from the window and the breath of fresh air, but by the time the bus rattled into Tsechow, she was covered with dust.

At the mission compound they were welcomed by a Mrs. Stanley Smith, not Mrs. Lawson, as Gladys had expected. Bewildered but grateful for Mrs. Smith's warm greetings, Gladys let herself be led into the mission.

"But where is Mrs. Lawson?" Gladys asked.

"She has gone to Yangcheng to minister to the people there. No one has ever gone that far into the mountains," Mrs. Smith continued, "but Jeannie Lawson wants to spend her last days witnessing to those who have never heard the gospel. Mr. Lu will take you there in a few days. However, it will be a hard trip by mule litter. You must rest first."

Gladys enjoyed the few days she stayed with Mrs. Smith. "What a pleasure it is to talk with an English lady again. You have made me feel just like your daughter."

"I'm glad," Mrs. Smith replied. "You don't know yet how we yearn for a face from home, but you will understand in time. That is, if you stay."

"Oh, I'll stay," Gladys replied confidently. "God has brought me this far. I wouldn't give up now."

The day Gladys left she shook out the folds of her orange dress and laughed. "This poor dress has had more wear in a month than most dresses have in a year!"

"Well, you won't be wearing it any more," Mrs. Smith said. She held up the clothes of a Chinese country woman. Gladys looked at the long robe in amazement.

"You will be traveling through rough country," Mrs. Smith said. "If bandits see you in a foreign dress, they will think you have money. You must wear this to be safe."

Gladys dressed in the Chinese robe. Looking down at herself, she couldn't help but laugh. "If Mum could see me now," she said.

"You look fine." Mrs. Smith smiled at the small woman. "Here, let me braid your hair."

When Gladys's long black hair was braided into one long braid hanging down her back, Mrs. Smith stepped back to look. "You look like a child. Are you sure you eat enough, Gladys?"

Gladys nodded. "I've always been thin. And always short," she added. "Mum said I stopped growing at five feet and that was that!"

"Well, you're strong enough, and that's what counts out here West of the Mountains," Mrs. Smith said.

"West of the Mountains?"

"Yes. This is Shansi province. It is called West of the Mountains." Mrs. Smith led the way outside.

"What a lovely name," Gladys murmured as she followed Mrs. Smith. "West of the Mountains. . . ." Her eyes lifted to the snowcapped peaks towering in the distance. "And that is Shansi too?"

Mrs. Smith nodded. "Yes, Shansi is a land of mountains and high valleys." She stopped in the courtyard of the mission where Mr. Lu waited beside a line of mules and coolies. The coolies carried long poles with baskets of grain at either end. Piled high with bundles, the mules stamped impatiently. A net litter had been strung between the two mules in front of the line. The litter was covered like a Conestoga wagon, and in it were Gladys's suitcases and other belongings. Mr. Lu stepped forward. "You will ride in the litter, Miss Aylward," he said, reaching to help her in.

Gladys climbed in carefully. The litter swayed, and she quickly realized that she would have to move carefully to keep it balanced. As she settled herself, Mrs. Smith said, "It has been so good to have you. Please come back to visit as soon as you can."

"Oh, yes," Gladys said. "And thank you so much."

There was a shouted command, and the mules began to move. Gladys waved until she had to catch the net to keep from being bounced out. Ahead of her rode Mr. Lu and the muleteers. Behind her came the coolies with their burdens.

Gladys sighed. "How nice not to have to carry everything myself this time."

Hours later she wasn't so sure. Already her muscles ached from being tossed back and forth in the net as they followed the mule track across the mountains.

At nightfall the caravan entered a walled city and stopped at an inn. Wearily, Gladys crawled out of the mule litter.

"We'll sleep here tonight," Mr. Lu told her. "The inn will be crowded. Few people dare to sleep outside the walls because of the bandits who roam the countryside."

Gladys nodded, too tired to speak. She followed him into the inn, barely listening as he spoke rapidly to the innkeeper. The innkeeper motioned toward a large room crowded with muleteers and coolies. Mr. Lu shook his head, took out his purse, and handed him a coin.

The innkeeper nodded, satisfied. He led Gladys to a small room away from the others. That night Gladys slept for the first time on a k'ang, the brick sleeping platform used by the Chinese. It was warmed by a small fire underneath the large, felt-covered platform. In the morning Gladys almost wished she didn't have to leave the cozy warmth of the k'ang. However, she was eager to meet Mrs. Lawson. Groaning, she stretched her aching muscles and crawled off the k'ang. After eating an early breakfast of boiled mullet and hot tea, Gladys and the men were on their way again.

The mule litter swung and dipped as the mountains rose higher. Gladys clutched the sides of the net as the mules' hooves clattered on the flinty trail. They traveled across barren, rocky slopes.

"It's like being at the top of the world," Gladys thought, looking down. In the distance on either side stretched blue-gray mountains. Down in the valleys, yellowish rivers twisted in long ribbons. The only sound was the occasional laugh or shout of a muleteer, or the sudden screech of a circling bird.

Late one afternoon, Gladys saw ahead of them a mountain covered with trees and bushes. Beyond it, a little higher, rose another mountain. Clinging to its side was a beautiful town. Its walls rose straight up from the flinty rock of the mountain. The stone gleamed in the last light of day. Minarets and towers, outlined by the setting sun, rose above the walls.

"It's a fairy-tale town," Gladys whispered, catching her breath. "Castles in the sky! How beautiful!"

The caravan plunged under the trees, the mules trotting quickly now. As they came back out into the sunlight, the town rose above them. Mr. Lu rode back to Gladys. "Yangcheng," he said, pointing. "The East Gate."

Gladys looked carefully. The road wound upward to a huge gate. Yes, Mrs. Smith had told her about the gates. Yangcheng had only two gates. The road ran right through the town. The muleteers and other travelers came in through one gate and went out through the other. At night both gates were closed, and no one was allowed to enter the city. Any latecomers stayed in the inns that lined the outside of the wall.

The caravan didn't enter the still open gate but turned down the road that bordered the wall. They wound past inns and courtyards and private houses. At one of the houses the caravan stopped.

"Mrs. Lawson," Mr. Lu said, pointing to the house.

Gladys unwound herself and painfully stood up. She stumbled to the door where Mr. Lu was banging loudly.

The door opened abruptly. A small white-haired woman stood in the open doorway.

"Come on in," Mrs. Lawson said. "Come on in!"

The Inn of the Eight Happinesses 5

Gladys took her bundles from the back of the mule and followed Mrs. Lawson. The big doors opened onto a gray-bricked courtyard. It looked somewhat like the inn Gladys had slept in the night before. It was square, enclosed by thick walls. Rooms lined the walls and opened out into the courtyard. A balcony ran along the upper story.

At one time it had been a pretty place. Now doors hung off their hinges, crumbled stone lay in the courtyard, and brooms leaned against the walls. Nothing resembled the neat missions Gladys had seen in Japan and on her way here.

Mrs. Lawson explained. "I just moved in," she said as she settled Gladys in the room next to hers. "Everyone thinks it's haunted, so I was able to rent it for almost nothing. I get a little money from home. It's enough to live on, but it won't get us a fancy house. We'll just have to clean this one up. It's big enough for a mission."

Gladys nodded, a little dazed and tired from her journey. She helped Mrs. Lawson sweep aside enough rubble to make room for a bedding roll to be spread on the k'ang. Then she reached for her bags.

"I know you're tired from your journey," Mrs. Lawson said. "You go on to bed. I'll help Mr. Lu find a room. I'll see you in the morning."

Gladys curled up on the bedding and opened her Bible. When she read in Psalm 34, "O magnify the Lord with me, and let us exalt his name together. I sought the Lord, and he heard me, and delivered me from all my fears," Gladys said a soft "Amen." She looked sleepily around the shadowy room. It was dirty, but comfortable. And dirt could always be cleaned up. Gladys vowed to go right to work the next day, helping all she could.

In the morning she awoke to the sound of rattling pots.

"Aiy-eee!" a strange voice called. A crash broke the morning quiet; then a cat sprang through Gladys's door and slid behind her bundles. It crouched, tail lashing, and watched the open door.

Gladys laughed and threw back her covers. She padded to the door. Only three downstairs rooms were being used—Mrs. Lawson's, Gladys's, and the one from which came loud yells and clattering.

Gladys peeked in. A Chinese man was quarreling to himself, straightening out the few pots he had. He wore a blue jacket and trousers, and his glossy black hair was braided into a queue that hung down his back. The queue swished angrily as he slammed a pot onto a stone ledge. Mrs. Lawson joined Gladys at the door, shaking her head.

"That cat's been in here again," she smiled. "This time he knocked everything off the shelf. Gladys, this is Yang, our cook."

Gladys nodded as Yang bowed in her direction and chattered in Chinese. Mrs. Lawson answered in the same language before she turned to Gladys. "You'll need to begin your study of Chinese today. No one here speaks English except me."

Gladys nodded uneasily, remembering the words of the mission chairman. "Months, years of study" echoed in her mind.

At breakfast they were joined by Mr. Lu. He was introduced to a beaming Yang, who filled their bowls with the broth and strings of boiled wheat dough common in northern China. After they had eaten and drunk their hot tea, Mr. Lu read the Bible, both in English and in Chinese. Yang was enthusiastic, nodding frequently and exclaiming as Mr. Lu read.

Later Mrs. Lawson offered to take Gladys into Yangcheng. She pushed open one of the

double doors to the street. As they stepped outside a group of children saw them and ran away, howling with fear.

"What are they saying?" Gladys asked in amazement.

"Foreign devil," Mrs. Lawson replied grimly. "That'll be the first word you learn. Most of these people have never seen a foreigner. Very few English people come this far into the mountains. When they get used to us, their fear will pass."

When the children were out of reach, they stopped and picked up handfuls of mud from the road. The mud flew through the air and spattered Gladys's clothes. At her sharp cry, Mrs. Lawson said, "That, too. I understand they are afraid of my white hair. Most Chinese hair turns gray as the people get older, not white. I usually come home covered from head to foot— with mud and other things too."

"But I love children," Gladys said regretfully. "I was looking forward to meeting them. They're beautiful children."

"They only do what they see their parents do," Mrs. Lawson said, brushing the mud from Gladys's gown. "They're just as lost as their parents. Don't worry. They are as curious as kittens. They'll be looking over your shoulder soon enough."

"How will we ever reach the people if they dislike us so?" Gladys winced as another mudball hit her between the shoulders.

"The Lord sent us here to give them the gospel. He'll find a way."

Mrs. Lawson began to walk toward the East Gate. Gladys gave up trying to clean her gown and followed. The huge gates of the town had been open since dawn. Inside, people were moving up and down the street. Mule trains, headed toward Tsechow, trotted by Gladys and Mrs. Lawson. As a camel caravan wound through the crowded street, Gladys stared. "Camels?"

"From the desert beyond the mountains," Mrs. Lawson explained. When Gladys still looked puzzled, she added, "The Gobi Desert."

"Oh," Gladys said, remembering something about the Gobi Desert from the classes at the missionary school. She watched the camels plod past. When they were gone she gave her attention to the shopkeepers calling from along the street. Even the dust couldn't dim the brass and silk glowing in the shops. The crisp air was fragrant with smoke and spices. A vendor squatted beside a cloth piled with dates, calling for customers. Another crouched beside a basket of golden persimmons. At one corner people clustered around a shadow show. Fascinated, Gladys watched the shadows of puppets dance behind the backlighted cloth. "Is it a holiday?" she asked.

Mrs. Lawson shook her head. "It's always like this. Yangcheng sits right on the trade route. The caravans go in one gate and out the other. There is no way around the town."

She stopped one of the little food wagons that were pulled along the street. She spoke rapidly to the vendor in Chinese. Then she reached into her purse and took out a coin. She handed it to the man and took two sticks threaded with crystallized, gingered grapes. The two women ate them one by one as they watched the caravans of mules, camels, and coolies wind through the streets.

"Do they all spend the night here?" Gladys asked.

"Most of them. Then they go on to other parts of China. They pass through here on the way home."

"Wouldn't it be wonderful to give them the gospel? Why, it would be taken to places we have never heard of!" Gladys exclaimed.

For a while they walked on in silence, ignoring the jeering shouts from the crowds. Then Mrs. Lawson caught Gladys's arm and stopped her.

"That's it!"

Startled, Gladys looked around. "What? What?"

"An inn! We'll open an inn!"

Gladys stared at Mrs. Lawson.

"Don't you see?" Mrs. Lawson continued. "It will be perfect! Our house used to be an inn. We will clean it up and open our own. We will feed the travelers, give them a place to sleep, and give them the gospel!"

The two women hurried back to the house, eager to get started. When they explained to Mr. Lu and Yang what they wanted to do, they had two excited helpers. Brooms whipped puffs of dust as they vigorously started to work. Yang repaired the doors and replaced the broken bricks. Mr. Lu went to find paper to fill the empty window frames. They all worked for several days before they stopped for an inspection.

Even the women were satisfied. The courtyard was clean and neat. Trees arched over the inn, making lacy patterns on the well-scrubbed bricks. Big pots had been placed about the courtyard, bringing color to the wintry scene. The bright tiled roof had been mended, new paper had been put in the windows, and the rooms were spotless.

"It's a miracle!" Gladys sighed happily.

Mrs. Lawson rubbed her aching back and gave Gladys a tired smile. "I agree it was a mess, but I didn't think it was that bad."

Yang shook his head as both women, older and younger, began to laugh. The ways of the foreign women were still strange to him. Strange but interesting.

"What will we call the inn?" Gladys asked. "The Red Lion or the White Boar sounds too English."

"We'll call it the Inn of the Eight Happinesses," Mrs. Lawson said, sitting down stiffly in a chair and rubbing her tired feet. "That sounds flowery enough to fit in with the names of the other inns along the road. Let's pray that it will bring the joy of God to others."

The next morning Mr. Lu had to return to Tsechow for a Bible meeting. By nightfall Gladys, Yang, and Mrs. Lawson were ready for their first customers. Long before dark the mule trains were entering the town. Some of them turned down the side road, seeking cheaper lodging.

None of them turned into the open doors of the Inn of the Eight Happinesses.

"Stand at the road and call out 'No bugs, no fleas,'" Mrs. Lawson said.

Gladys gave her a startled look.

"That's what the others are doing." Mrs. Lawson made Gladys repeat the Chinese words until she got them right.

So Gladys stood at the road, hands tucked into her jacket, calling, "No bugs! No fleas!"

By nightfall not one muleteer had entered the foreign devils' inn.

"This calls for drastic action," Mrs. Lawson said thoughtfully. She turned to Gladys, "You'll have to do it. You're younger and stronger. Besides, one look at my white hair and they'll run."

"Do what?" Gladys asked, puzzled.

"Grab the lead mule and pull him into the courtyard. The others will follow. Then we will have the muleteers!"

Gladys swallowed hard. The mules were big. They had never looked tame to her, not even when she rode on the mule litter. "All right," she said faintly, and walked back to the road.

Carefully she watched each train, hoping to find a small mule. At last she gave up and decided to take the very next train. "Don't let the mule bite, Lord," she prayed as the lead mule plodded out of the darkness.

As Gladys lunged forward she saw that she

had picked the biggest mule yet to pass. It was too late to jump back. Gladys missed the mule's harness and stumbled past the mule. The muleteers took one look at the white face turned toward them. They leaped off the mules and disappeared down the street, shrieking with fear.

Turning, Gladys grabbed the big mule firmly and led the train into the courtyard.

"I lost the men," she called to a laughing Mrs. Lawson. "They ran away!"

"They'll be back," Mrs. Lawson replied, wiping tears of laughter from her eyes. "Oh, Gladys, you were marvelous!"

The men did return for their mules. They came to stay the night at the Inn of the Eight Happinesses, as did many others later. After Yang had carried the last bowl back into the kitchen, Mrs. Lawson sat on a stool in front of the men and sang a song. The men listened quietly at first, then hesitantly joined in. After they sang the song twice, Mrs. Lawson opened her Bible. Gladys sat down near the door and watched the men's faces as Mrs. Lawson began speaking in Chinese.

"Long ago a man called Jesus Christ lived in Nazareth. . . ."

The Mandarin 6

"Lai . . . lai . . . ai!"

Gladys slammed the Chinese textbook shut and tossed it on the table. She had always had difficulty keeping her mind on her studies, and today it was especially hard. A soft breeze beckoned her through the courtyard and out the gates of the inn.

Spring came early to the bleak mountain ranges of Shansi that first year. It spread a haze of green foliage over the rocky slopes nearest Yangcheng. The lacy shadows of plum trees danced over the dirt road outside the inn. Gladys walked slowly along the road. She waved to one passerby and called out in Chinese to another.

Throughout the long winter, when snow had blanketed the mountains and blocked the passes, Yang had taught Gladys the Chinese language.

The neighbors, finally used to seeing the foreign women, had helped. They were eager to teach their ways to the smiling young woman who stopped to play with their children.

Now Gladys could pass children playing in the street without fear of flying mudballs. They, too, had discovered the "storytellers" who ran the Inn of the Eight Happinesses. Time erased their fear of the "foreign devils." They ran beside Gladys, laughing and calling, "Tell us a story!"

Smiling, Gladys began a simple version of Noah and the ark as she walked. The children walked beside her, listening eagerly.

Cheerfully, Gladys greeted each passerby. Listening and repeating what she heard gave her an understanding of the difficult Chinese language that no book ever could. Whenever Gladys went into Yangcheng on an errand, she took one or two of the children with her. They escorted her to stores and to the tea shops. Gladys listened carefully as the children and shopkeepers argued over prices. In this way, day after day, she practiced her Chinese while going about her daily chores.

Mr. Lu had returned to the inn after the spring thaw. He preached to the muleteers as Mrs. Lawson traveled to the villages close to Yangcheng. Gladys went with her. As they entered the gates of each village, the two small women were usually greeted with jeers. At first Gladys was nervous and looked to Mrs. Lawson for help. Mrs. Lawson did not hesitate. She knew that the villagers would give up if she didn't show fear. Gladys discovered that Mrs. Lawson was right. When Mrs. Lawson began to sing in Chinese, the villagers gathered around to listen. They stayed to listen to the stories.

At village after village, Mrs. Lawson told the gospel story to the people. As Gladys listened, she memorized some of the words. When she had learned enough words to present a short parable, Mrs. Lawson asked her to speak to the people. As Gladys told the simple story, she was delighted at the response of the people gathered around her.

"This is what God sent me to do," Gladys thought with pleasure. She worked harder than ever. The inn became a success. At times, six or seven teams of mules were tied in the courtyard. The rooms upstairs and downstairs were packed with muleteers.

For almost a year, life went on in this manner. As Gladys became better at speaking Chinese, she translated her favorite choruses. Often when Mr. Lu was gone, Mrs. Lawson spoke to the men. Sometimes Gladys took Mrs. Lawson's place and told one of the gospel stories.

Then one day Gladys's life changed. While Mrs. Lawson was staying at another inn, she fell from a twenty-foot-high balcony. The innkeeper sent for Gladys. When she arrived, Mrs. Lawson was delirious, suffering from a broken spine. For over two months Gladys nursed the woman she had grown to love and respect.

One night she heard Mrs. Lawson recite softly,
Come unto me, all ye that labour and
are heavy laden, and I will give you rest.
Take my yoke upon you, and learn of
me; for I am meek and lowly in heart:
and ye shall find rest unto your souls.
For my yoke is easy, and my burden is
light.

When Gladys went in to check on Mrs. Lawson, the older woman whispered, "God sent you to take my place. Never give up, Gladys. Never give up."

At noon the next day Mrs. Lawson died. Gladys was alone in a strange land, without money and without the wisdom and strength of the older woman.

"What will we do?" Yang asked.

"I won't give up," Gladys said stubbornly. "The rent is paid for the rest of the year. Mr. Lu will be back in a few weeks. We'll keep the inn open."

"You must speak to the Mandarin," Yang said. "He rules this land. He will know what to do."

"I've never seen a Mandarin in my life," Gladys said. "I wouldn't know what to say."

Yang shook his head and shuffled back into the kitchen. Gladys could hear him banging pots and muttering.

A few weeks later Gladys was cleaning the upstairs rooms when she heard a shout. She looked over the balcony. Yang ran through the door, shouting, "The Mandarin is coming! The Mandarin is coming!" He gave Gladys a frightened look and disappeared into the kitchen.

Gladys tucked the straggling strands of hair back into her bun and brushed off her skirt. "He could have let me know," she snapped. Annoyed and embarrassed at being caught in such a mess, she marched down the stairs and into the courtyard.

When a line of people entered the courtyard, Gladys forgot her sharp words. She stood still, amazed. Coolies carried a sedan chair curtained in silk. On either side walked the Mandarin's clerks, dressed in dark blue robes. Other servants followed at a respectable distance.

A clerk stepped forward and opened the door of the sedan. The Mandarin stepped out. He was tall and had the pale ivory face of a man who spent his time indoors. Gleaming black hair hung in a queue down his back, and a long, glossy mustache drooped at the corners of his mouth. His long-sleeved gown, brightly embroidered with flowers and birds, fell smoothly to pointed, black silk shoes.

"I have come to ask your advice," the Mandarin said.

"Oh!" Gladys murmured.

"You are aware that for many generations foot-binding has been practiced in this province?" he asked.

"Has it?" Gladys closed her eyes. When she opened them, the Mandarin was still there. He frowned at her.

"The feet of females are bound soon after they are born," he said.

"Oh!" Gladys said again.

"We have a decree from the Central Government that this practice must stop," the Mandarin continued. "Every woman in this province has bound feet. Therefore, someone with big, unbound feet must do the job of inspection."

Gladys didn't dare look down at her own feet.

"No man can undertake this job. It is not right for a man to look at the bare feet of a woman.

You must find a woman from another province to do the job."

Gladys nodded.

"The job does not pay well. The wages are one measure of grain a day and three cash to buy vegetables. A mule will be supplied to make the journey into the country, and two soldiers will go as guards. You will find such a woman?"

"I will do my best," Gladys said faintly, and bowed. The Mandarin stepped back into the sedan and left the courtyard.

Gladys asked the muleteers who stopped at the inn if they knew of such a woman. They shook their heads. Two months later the Mandarin was back.

"Where is the woman?" he asked.

"I tried, but there was no one . . ." Gladys began.

The Mandarin gave her a stern look. "Then you will take the job."

"Me!"

"Of course," he replied. "You are the only one who has big feet!"

Suddenly Gladys realized what this could mean to her ministry. She took a deep breath. "You know that I will make every effort to win the villagers to Christ?"

There was sudden silence in the courtyard. When the Mandarin spoke, his voice was quiet. "I care nothing for your religion. Every man must choose as he sees fit."

"Then I accept the job," Gladys said. She gave a sigh of relief when the courtyard was empty again.

When Mr. Lu returned from Tsechow, he agreed to continue preaching at the inn. Yang was delighted with the opportunity to run the inn himself. Gladys was free to begin her new job. Inspecting feet kept her busy. She went into every house in Yangcheng and the neighboring villages. The soldiers rode in front of her. In each village the soldiers called cheerfully, "Unbind feet or go to prison!"

Over the months that followed, Gladys went farther and farther back into the mountains. In every house she told the story of Christ.

Many of the villages were just clusters of mud houses clinging to the mountains where a patch of ground was good for growing crops. Few outsiders reached their gates. Gladys's visits became occasions of celebration at which she was the guest of honor. The villagers listened to her songs and stories eagerly. Soon they were calling her "the storyteller."

Spring rains filled the gorges and gullies, sending water rushing in torrents down the rocky slopes. Fall brought cold winds, and frost iced the tiled temple roofs. When the winds came from the north, icicles hung from the upturned eaves of the pagodas, and winter again blanketed the land in a snowy cocoon. Everyone sought the warmth of his own k'ang until spring came once again.

Gladys was one of the first out after the spring thaw. She rode her mule back into the mountains, escorted by the Mandarin's soldiers. Going about the Mandarin's business meant that Gladys was also going about the Lord's business. Her circle of converts grew daily.

A few Christians here, a few Christians there, and a small church was started in one of the villages. Since Gladys could not return often to the same village, the converts chose one of their members to become their pastor. Over the next two years, the number of small churches increased across the countryside. It was not uncommon for Gladys to hear one of the choruses she usually taught sung by a complete stranger passing through the crowded streets of Yangcheng. Nor was it unusual for strangers to seek out the Inn of the Eight Happinesses, asking for the woman they called "the storyteller."

Gladys rejoiced in the simple faith of the villagers, but sometimes she had doubts about her work. She wondered, "Do they really understand? Could their faith stand being put to the test?"

The Riot 7

Gladys didn't realize how soon her own faith would be put to the test. One day a messenger arrived from the governor.

"There's a riot in the prison," the messenger cried. "You must come!"

Gladys shook her head. "What could I do? That's a job for a man."

"You must come! It is the governor's order!"

The frightened messenger insisted until Gladys agreed to go see what was the matter. When she arrived at the prison, the governor was waiting outside.

His face was pale. "Listen," he said nervously.

Gladys didn't need to listen. She had heard the yells and shrieks as she walked up the hill.

"The prisoners are killing each other," the governor said. He placed his hands into his wide sleeves and tried to look at Gladys with authority. "You must stop them."

"Me?" Gladys gasped. "Why me?"

"The guards are afraid. You must do something."

"I am only a missionary woman," she said. "What could I do? Send for the soldiers."

"I did, but they are frightened. There are not enough of them," the governor replied. "You must go inside the prison and stop the riot."

"Are you crazy? They would kill me!"

"How could they kill you?" the governor said simply. "You say you have the living God inside you."

"The living God?"

"You have gone throughout our towns and villages preaching about the living God. You say He is with you always. If your words are true, then you can stop this riot."

For a moment Gladys didn't speak. The governor was right. If she didn't trust God now, she would never again be able to reach these people for Christ.

"Let me in," she said quietly, her face now as pale as the governor's.

The governor produced a huge key and opened the door. Trembling, Gladys stepped inside. The door slammed behind her, and she heard the key turn in the lock.

Gladys stood in the entrance to a long tunnel. Far down the tunnel she could see men running about wildly in a courtyard. Gladys felt like Daniel in the lions' den. The thought gave her courage. "God sealed the lions' mouths," she thought. "He is able to do the same for me. Somehow this will work for the glory of God."

She took a step forward. "My God is able to deliver me," she whispered, taking another step. Softly she began to sing in a breathless voice,

> A mighty fortress is our God,
> A bulwark never failing;
> Our helper He, amid the flood
> Of mortal ills prevailing.

At the end of the tunnel she stopped. The sight that met her eyes was worse than she had imagined. The courtyard was about sixty feet square. Cages of bamboo lined the walls. Several bloodstained bodies were stretched out on the hard-packed clay ground. As she watched in horror, a group of men rushed across the courtyard. They were followed by a man swinging an axe.

Gladys gasped as he charged toward the men. They scattered, each man running for his life. The man with the axe chased the slowest one toward Gladys. Just in front of Gladys the terrified runner swerved aside. Gladys was left facing the man with the axe.

Suddenly Gladys was furiously angry. She took two steps forward and shouted, "Give me that axe!"

The man stopped short and stared at Gladys.
She reached forward and took the axe, letting
it hang loosely from her hand.

"The rest of you," she screamed. "Line up
in front of me!"

The prisoners slowly filed toward her and
formed a line. Gladys looked at the dirty, miserable
faces. Her fear disappeared.

"You should be ashamed of yourselves," she
scolded. "What is the meaning of all this?"

When they looked at each other and didn't answer, Gladys said, "Appoint a spokesman. I intend to find out just what is going on here."

One man was chosen. He stepped forward.

"The rest of you clean up this mess," Gladys demanded, pointing to the bloody bodies. "I'll deal with you later."

She turned toward the spokesman. "Now, tell me what happened."

"We are given an axe for an hour a day to cut up our food," the man said, "but the only food we have is what our relatives send us. Not everyone gets food. It is hard to watch others eat when you are starving. Things got out of hand. We are sorry."

Gladys looked at the thin, scrawny bodies of the men. "Not enough food?" The men nodded in agreement.

"What do you do in here all day?" Gladys asked.

"Nothing," the men replied.

Gladys heard a sound behind her. She turned to see the governor and the soldiers coming through the tunnel. The governor gave Gladys a look of awe. "You have worked a miracle," he said.

"Not I," Gladys replied, "but my God. He is the only One who works miracles."

"Yes, the Living God is powerful indeed," the governor exclaimed.

"You must give these men food," Gladys demanded. "Some of them are starving!"

The governor nodded. "It will be done."

"And give them something to do. They must not sit idle all day with nothing to occupy their minds and hands."

"Yes, Ai-weh-deh," the governor said as Gladys handed him the bloody axe. "It shall be done as you say."

When Gladys returned home, she asked Yang what "Ai-weh-deh" meant.

"It means 'the Virtuous One,'" he replied. From that time on, Gladys was called Ai-weh-deh by the Chinese people. They had always admired Gladys's courage and kindness, but after all, she was only a woman. When she stopped the riot, she was regarded with respect. The Living God who had enabled her to do such an impossible deed was regarded with awe.

Gladys found that the Chinese people were even more interested in the gospel than ever before. When she realized why, she remembered the thought that had crossed her mind before she entered that long, dark tunnel: "Somehow this will work for the glory of God." And so it had.

The Children 8

One day as Gladys walked through the crowded streets of Yangcheng, she saw a woman sitting on the side of the road. The woman was filthy, but silver earrings dangled from her ears, and ornaments of jade gleamed in her hair. When Gladys stopped to speak to the woman, she saw a child leaning against the woman's knee.

The child's belly was huge, bloated from lack of food. Its head and body were so covered with running sores that Gladys couldn't tell if it was a boy or a girl.

Sick with horror, Gladys said sternly, "Woman, you shouldn't sit on the street with a child in that condition!"

"The child is no concern of yours," the woman replied sharply.

"Oh, yes, it is!" Gladys was angry. "I am Ai-weh-deh, the foot inspector! If that child stays in this sun much longer, it will die!"

"So what if it does? I'll soon get another one," the woman said, laughing at Gladys.

"You can't be that child's mother," Gladys said sharply. "You don't have a mother's love!"

When the woman spoke again, Gladys realized what she was.

"If you're so concerned, I'll let you have the child for two dollars," the woman offered.

"You're a child dealer! You buy and sell children!"

"Two dollars," the woman grinned, leaning back against the wall.

Gladys walked away in disgust. The woman's harsh laughter followed her. Around the corner, Gladys walked up the wide steps of the yamen, the Mandarin's palace. Inside, she waited impatiently until she was taken to see the Mandarin.

After greeting him, she spoke quickly. "What do you do with dealers in children?"

"I do not understand you."

"A few yards away from this palace, a woman tried to sell me a child for two dollars!" Gladys's outrage was plain to see.

The Mandarin was unhappy. For a time he didn't speak. Gladys could almost see him choosing words and then discarding them. At last he spoke bluntly. "Nothing."

"Nothing . . ." Gladys couldn't hide her disappointment. The usually wise Mandarin had failed her.

"If she is a child dealer, as you say, then she is a member of a terrible band of criminals. It would bring disaster to Yangcheng if I interfered in any way. The criminals would not hesitate to murder us in our sleep."

As Gladys turned to leave, the Mandarin stopped her with an uplifted hand. "The law says that Ai-weh-deh must walk on the other side of the street. You must not look at the woman or the child. And you will not repeat my words to anyone. Go!"

In the doorway Gladys turned back to look with angry eyes at the man she respected. Standing as tall as she could, eyes flashing, she spoke calmly and clearly.

"I did not come to China only to observe your laws. I came for the love of Jesus Christ, and I shall act upon the principles of His teaching!"

If the huge doorway could have been slammed, Gladys would have slammed it. As it was, she spun on her heels and left, her head held high.

When Gladys approached the woman and child, the woman called out, "Lady with the heart of pity! Buy the child!"

"I don't have two dollars," Gladys said, frowning down at her.

"Then I will sell it for one and a half," the woman wheedled.

"Don't have it," Gladys snapped.

"Then how much do you have?" the woman asked.

Gladys reached into her jacket pocket. She pulled out all the Chinese coins that she had and handed them to the woman. "Here is all I have!"

"She's yours," the woman said. She stood up quickly and shuffled off down the street. Gladys stood looking down at the child she had just bought for ninepence. Then she took her by the hand and led her home.

When they reached the inn, the child ran to the darkest corner and crouched, terrified.

Yang stared, and then shook his head in disgust. "She will soon die," he said.

"She's hungry, Yang," Gladys said. "Bring her some food."

Yang placed a bowl of millet near the child. When he stepped back, the child rushed out of the corner, grabbed the bowl, and retreated. Gladys and Yang watched as she scooped the food out with her fingers and stuffed it into her mouth.

"See," Gladys said triumphantly. "She won't die!"

And she didn't. As the months passed the child grew into a healthy little girl, although she was smaller than she might have been if she had been fed properly. She was somewhere between four and six years old. Lively and cheerful, she skipped

around the inn as if she had always been there. Gladys named her "Beautiful Grace," but she always called her Ninepence, for that had been her price.

Yang soon gave up his predictions of trouble and became the little girl's devoted friend. Even the battle-scarred old cat that sometimes raided Yang's kitchen fell under the spell of her charm. He allowed Ninepence to carry him around and could often be found curled up on her warm k'ang for a midday nap.

Ninepence brought great joy to Gladys. Gladys had always loved children and longed to have her own. It had taken her some time to accept the fact that it wasn't God's will for her to marry and have children. Now she was thankful for this bright child the Lord had given her. What a pleasure the quiet winter evenings became as Gladys's stories made the people of the Bible come alive for Ninepence. What happiness it gave Gladys to hear her songs echoed by the light voice of a child. What excitement it was to see her own child respond to the Word of God, for Ninepence's mind was as lively as her body, and she was quick to learn.

It was Ninepence who brought the next child. One night, near suppertime, she appeared at Gladys's elbow. "Is supper ready?" she asked.

"Almost," Gladys answered, smiling at the bright-eyed little girl.

"Is it good?" Ninepence swung around to peer into Gladys's face.

"Of course," Gladys laughed. "Run and play. I'll call you when Yang is ready."

Ninepence lingered. "If I eat a little less tonight, would you eat a little less?"

"I suppose," Gladys replied, puzzled. "But why?"

"Well, if we put the two lesses in a bowl, there would be enough for one more."

"Ninepence, what are you up to?"

Ninepence smiled, her eyes sparkling. "There's someone outside who could use a little 'less' in his bowl."

Gladys followed her outside. A small, quiet boy stood bravely in the street. He didn't look much better than Ninepence had when Gladys first saw her. Ninepence had found him begging on the streets. The boy was eight years old, old enough to tell Gladys his story. Bandits had raided his village. They had killed the men and taken the women. His mother had died in a ditch. The boy had wandered from village to village, begging whatever food he could get.

He ate his first meal with them that night, and he stayed for ten years. His nickname was Less.

One day Gladys took her dirty clothes to the riverbank to wash them. She dipped a jacket into the water, pulled it out, and pounded it with a rock. As she pounded, she sang. Her clear voice covered the noise of the children's steps. Gladys looked up and was startled to see them behind her on the bank. Between them, holding to their hands, was a smiling two-year-old boy.

"Who's that?" Gladys asked, pushing damp hair out of her eyes.

"We don't know." Ninepence replied. "We just found him."

"You found him? Well, take him back to his mother. Quickly!" Gladys turned back to her washing.

"There is no mother," Less said. "We looked."

"Can we keep him?" Ninepence asked eagerly.

"No, indeed!" Gladys was on her feet in a second. "Do you think I want to be accused of child stealing?"

She ran up and down the river bank, calling. No one answered. There was nothing to do but take the child to the yamen. The Mandarin inquired of the townspeople, but no one knew the child.

"What shall I do with him?" Gladys asked.

"Keep him," the Mandarin replied. "He is yours."

"A two-year-old!"

The Mandarin shrugged and didn't answer. That was the way Precious Bundle became part of Gladys's growing household.

That was only the beginning. Others came. They were left in the streets, or sent to the town with instructions to ask for Ai-weh-deh, the Virtuous One. "God supplied me a family out of his abundance," Gladys was to say many years later. "I had no one of my own to love, and He sent me many."

By now Gladys had been completely accepted by the Chinese people. She spoke Chinese, even some of the dialects, very well. So completely had she accepted China as the place where God wanted her to be that she thought and dreamed in Chinese. But still Gladys felt that one thing stood between her and the people. They were Chinese by nationality; she was English. Gladys decided to give up her British passport and apply for citizenship in China. She received her papers as a naturalized Chinese in 1936, only four years after arriving in China. "Now," she said, "I am truly one with the people God gave me."

Teaching the growing number of children at the inn became a problem. As much as Gladys enjoyed both the children and the teaching, there just weren't enough hours in the day. Besides, her job as foot inspector took her away from the inn for weeks at a time. The Mandarin solved the problem. A school was provided for both the children at the inn and for the children of the town officials.

The friendship between the Mandarin and Gladys had grown over the years. They had spent many hours in his yamen discussing the customs of China. The Mandarin explained the Chinese idea of a "Princely Man" to Gladys.

"But no man is perfect," Gladys disagreed. "What about your wars, and these abandoned children? How can you say that Chinese men are becoming perfect?"

"Eventually the perfect man will exist," the Mandarin replied, folding his arms in his wide sleeves. "We have only to be patient."

"We believe that there was only one perfect man, Jesus Christ, the Son of the Living God. He died for us so that we, believing on Him, might have eternal life. Only through Him will we ever be perfect, and that not in this life." Gladys leaned forward earnestly. Her lack of education bothered her in these sessions with such an intelligent man. "If only I knew more," she would think, "then perhaps I could reach him."

In the countryside and in the towns the kindly peasants listened and believed. The number of converts at the inn grew under the ministry of Mr. Lu, who divided his time between the

Yangcheng mission and the one at Tsechow.

Mr. Lu had gone to Tsechow the day the planes came out of the east. Gladys was in an upstairs room at the inn, praying with Yang and four converts. When the people of the village heard the unfamiliar roar of the planes, they ran out into the streets to look up in the sky. They stood there, waving and shouting at the pretty silver planes. The planes swept over the town once, twice, and released their bombs. For Gladys, the whole world seemed to turn upside down and plunge into darkness. And in the darkness was the sound of weeping.

War 9

The weeping was the first sound Gladys heard. She opened her eyes slowly. Dust filled the air, and she could barely see. Carefully she moved her arms and legs. Something was pressing down on her back. She stopped struggling and lay still.

Gladys had heard the rumors of war, as had the others of Yangcheng. But as the villagers had said, what are rumors but puffs of wind?

"Hardly a puff of wind," Gladys thought grimly. The floor of the upstairs prayer room had collapsed. It had fallen to the room below, burying Gladys, Yang, and the converts under broken brick, tile, and wood.

When rescuers arrived, they pulled Gladys from under a broken beam. Shaken, she crawled over the rubble to a pale Less and tearful Ninepence, who had watched the rescue. A quick

glance told Gladys that they were not hurt.

"The other children? How are the children?" she asked.

"They are all right," Less replied quickly. "The bomb hit just this corner of the inn. We had run outside to watch the planes. A few of the little ones have scratches and bruises. They are mostly scared."

"You two help take care of them until the rescue work is done," Gladys said. "Don't worry. God will take care of you, and I'll be with you as soon as I can."

She smiled at the other children now gathering in the opening. "Go, go," she said, motioning them away. She stood for a moment, watching Less lead them away with quiet confidence unusual in a child of his age. Ninepence followed, her usually bright eyes solemn under her straight bangs. She held Precious Bundle too tightly, as if that were the only way she could keep him safe.

Sighing, Gladys turned back to help Yang dig out the last man.

"How is the rest of the town?" Gladys asked.

"It is dreadful, dreadful!" replied one of the rescuers. "Everything is broken, all are killed!"

Gladys got her small medicine chest from her untouched room and hurried to the East Gate. The walls and gate were untouched, but nothing in her life had prepared Gladys for what she saw past the gate.

The center of the town was completely destroyed. The main street was littered with bricks, plaster, and broken stone. Bodies were scattered throughout the rubble, and those who were still alive screamed for help. The ones who had escaped injury were running about in despair.

Horror swept over Gladys and held her still for a moment. Then, stepping forward, she called hoarsely to the survivors, "Bring water! Clear the main street! Take the dead outside the city, do you hear?"

"Yes, Ai-weh-deh!"

Gladys went from one person to the next. She bandaged those who were hurt. By late afternoon she had worked only three-quarters of the way up the street. On a corner beside the palace an old man sat holding his head. As Gladys crawled over broken stone to reach him, he looked up.

"So God is still alive," he said, "You're still here."

"I'm not God," Gladys replied sharply. "And they can't kill Him, ever! Why aren't you helping?"

"I only stopped for a moment." The old man pointed at the palace. "We're all working there."

Gladys looked toward the palace and saw the governor working with a crew of men. When she reached him, he gave her a tired smile.

"I knew that if you were alive, you would be doing everything you could to help the people, Ai-weh-deh," he said. "We're putting the wounded in the palace."

"Where is the Mandarin?" Gladys asked.

"Come with me," the governor replied. He led the way into the palace where the Mandarin was working.

Gladys was surprised when she saw the Mandarin. He had both silk sleeves pushed back, and he was working with guards and officials to help the wounded.

"Ai-weh-deh!" he exclaimed, "You are hurt!"

Until then Gladys had given no thought to how she looked. Then she realized that her gown had been torn by the broken beam and the rubble. She was covered with dirt and filth, and streaked with the blood of those she had helped. She shook her head wearily, "No, I'm not hurt. A bomb destroyed only one corner of the inn. My children were not hurt. They are safe."

"For now," the Mandarin said grimly. I have news that the Japanese have conquered the city of Luan and are marching toward Tsechow. They will come to Yangcheng next. We must finish our work here and leave Yangcheng before they arrive."

"The muleteers can help," Gladys suggested.

The Mandarin nodded. "The wounded can be taken to the Buddhist temple. It was unharmed, and so was the temple of Lang Quai. The homeless can stay there."

"And the dead?"

"A pit will be dug in the ancient cemetery outside the West Gate," the Mandarin replied. "The dead will be buried there. When the work is done everyone must leave the city."

"Where will you go?" Gladys asked.

"To the mountains," the Mandarin answered, "until it is safe to return here. Will you come with us?"

Gladys thought a moment. "No," she said slowly. "I will go to Bei Chai Chuang. I have visited there often, and we will be welcome there. It is a hard village to find. Bei Chai Chuang will be a safe place for my children."

That night the flickering light of many lanterns lit the streets of Yangcheng as the rescue work went on.

Gladys was the last to finish. She left the city and walked wearily down the road past the houses and other inns. The gates of the Inn of the Eight Happinesses stood open. Worried, Gladys began to hurry. Inside, she found the children not only safe and well, but ready to leave Yangcheng. Christians from the city and surrounding homes had gathered in the courtyard. "We will go with you, Ai-weh-deh," they said.

Gladys nodded. The other villagers had left for the mountains, finding shelter in remote villages and towns. Gladys took her children and the Christians of Yangcheng to Bei Chai Chuang. Bei Chai Chuang was an isolated village southwest of Yangcheng. It could be reached only by traveling over a hidden rocky trail. In all the time Gladys was to stay there, the village was never discovered by the Japanese.

Five days after the people left Yangcheng, the Japanese marched from Tsechow and entered the East Gate of Yangcheng to find a deserted city.

In the mountains the people waited and watched. When word finally reached Gladys that the Japanese had left Yangcheng, she decided to go back after the box of deeds and important papers that she had left in the inn. She walked warily down the western trail toward Yangcheng. When she reached the walled city, the West Gates were closed. Crawling over barriers, she followed the wall around the city. When she reached the

East Gate she turned down the street that ran along the wall.

The deserted houses huddled against the wall, their doors opening onto empty courtyards. A sudden movement in an overturned cart sent Gladys's heart racing. Then the old cat appeared over the side of the cart, holding a rat in its mouth.

"So you're still here," Gladys said, shaky with relief. "Ninepence will be happy for you, at least."

Gladys turned into the alleyway leading to the Inn of the Eight Happinesses. She heard the inn sign creaking in the wind. The inn was just as they had left it, the bombed corner open to the sky. Gladys stood for a moment looking at it and thinking of the last six years. Then, impatient with herself, she marched into the courtyard. The box had been in the upstairs room. Gladys scratched in the rubble left by the bomb. It took her a while to find the box. As she lifted it out, a twig snapped behind her. She whirled, her hand to her throat.

"Scared you, didn't I?"

Gladys frowned. She recognized the water carrier, an old man with a sly face. He was a thief and had probably stayed behind to loot the houses.

"The Japanese are coming back," he grinned, looking at the box in her hands.

"I don't believe you," Gladys said, turning away.

"But they are at the West Gate now." His voice dropped to a hoarse whisper. "You'd better leave."

"Nonsense!" Gladys snapped. At that moment there was an explosion from the direction of the West Gate. Frightened, Gladys dropped the box and ran.

Behind her she heard the evil chuckling of the old man. "It won't do you any good," he called after her. "The gates are barred!"

As Gladys ran she heard other explosions. When she reached the East Gate, it was locked and barred, just as the old man had said. Frantically she looked behind her. To the east lay the city of Tsechow, surely in enemy hands. The only safe place for Gladys was Bei Chai Chuang. But that mountain village lay to the southwest, past the West Gate.

Gladys had no choice. Cautiously, she scrambled back around the wall to the West Gate. Beneath the gate Japanese soldiers lay sprawled behind rocks, firing up at Chinese Nationalist soldiers inside the city. The Chinese were firing back and tossing down hand grenades.

Gladys bit her lip. She had to get past the battle. Between her and the soldiers was the ancient graveyard where they had buried the dead from the bombing. Gladys slipped from tombstone to tombstone, staying behind the soldiers. Then she dashed into a field of green wheat and crawled until she reached the mountain slope.

There she was faced with two choices. She could take the quick, easy way through the dry stream bed, or the harder, rocky path cut from the mountainside.

"Help me, Lord," she prayed. "Help me choose the safe way."

Gladys took the rocky path. About half a mile farther on, she heard the sound of marching feet. Looking down, she saw Japanese troops coming down the dry stream bed. Had she taken that way, she would have been captured, if not killed.

Gladys gave thanks silently for the watchful care of her Lord as she hurried toward Bei Chai Chuang. Once there she explained to her flock of Christians and the villagers what had happened. They refused to let her go again. Day after day, the men from Bei Chai Chuang went out to check on the movements of the Japanese. Gladys remained behind, starting Bible classes with the villagers. Her group of forty Christians from Yangcheng worshiped with her village friends. Not even a war could stop the Lord's work. Then, too, there were the children. Gladys gathered them together and began teaching them. She translated hymns and choruses for them to learn in Chinese.

One day a messenger reported, "The Japanese are gone. The gates of Yangcheng are open, and the town crier is outside calling for people to come back and clear their courtyards."

"Clear the courtyards . . . but we cleared them

before we left." Gladys thought for a moment about the battle she had witnessed and the marching troops she had seen on the western trail. "You stay here," she said to her people. "I will go back and see."

The messenger took her back to Yangcheng. There was an air of emptiness about the town. No one moved outside the walls. No smoke curled above the town. Gladys and the messenger walked slowly through the gates. Again bodies lay in the streets, this time shot or bayoneted. Gladys couldn't even weep. "Twice," she thought. "Twice in such a short time."

She saw some people crowded around the entrance to the palace. Inside, she found the Mandarin. His face was gray, his eyes sick with horror.

"I came back this morning," he said. "And this is what I found."

"We must bury them quickly," Gladys said, her voice flat and dull.

He nodded, getting up wearily. "It will be done."

As they worked, he told Gladys what had happened. It was as she had suspected. The refugees who had come back first had been caught in the battle. Not one, soldier or refugee, had been left alive.

When the burials were finished, Gladys walked out of Yangcheng. On a mountaintop she stopped to look back at the city. Its strong walls still reached upwards, shadowing the destruction that lay inside. But Gladys knew that nothing could erase the memory of what she had seen. The peaceful, contented days of Yangcheng were over. The land that Gladys had grown to love was a battlefield.

The Scorched Earth 10

The walls of Bei Chai Chuang had been built to fit smoothly into the mountainside. From a distance they looked just like part of the mountain itself. The mountains towered above the village, and below the village the slope fell sharply down. In the center of the walled village there was a cave in the mountainside. In the peaceful past, it had been used for stabling animals. Now, clean and neat, it was a hospital.

Gladys woke just after dawn. Moving carefully so that she wouldn't wake the sleeping children, she dressed. Then she hurried across the balcony and down the stone steps to the kitchen. She prepared a bowlful of millet and drank some twig tea. Ninepence and Sualan, another of Gladys's girls, came in to help prepare the children's breakfast.

"Good morning, Mother," Ninepence said. She and Sualan stopped to give Gladys a kiss. Gladys hugged them both and watched them go to the rough stone ledge where Gladys's fire still burned. Sualan was only a year older than Ninepence, but she moved with a grace learned at the Mandarin's palace, where she had been a slave girl. Ninepence was no longer a child, but she still had the glowing liveliness that had made her as charming then as she was now. Gladys listened with pleasure to the laughter and chatter of the girls as they worked. They had taken over Yang's duties as cook. Yang had returned to his own village to wait out the war. Gladys had not heard from him since he left.

Gladys put her blue patterned bowl down on the table and stood up. "Yang is not the only one we haven't heard from," she thought. Since the war had begun, no mail had arrived from home. Gladys wondered if any of her letters had even left China.

Outside the house the mountain air was crisp and cool. Gladys paused for a moment to look across the deep valley to the distant mountain peaks. "Such beauty," she thought. "Only God could create such beauty."

Her heart lifted in praise for the Creator of all things. When she entered the cave hospital a few minutes later, she was able to greet her ten patients cheerfully as usual.

"Hello, Francis," she whispered to a sleepy-eyed child. "How's my boy?"

Francis smiled although his eyes were clouded with pain. He cradled the hand that had only two remaining fingers. Francis was one of Gladys's new children. Her family was growing rapidly. She had brought many children with her from Yangcheng. Less, Ninepence, Timothy, Sualan, Precious Bundle, Crystal, Precious Jade, Wan Yu, Pearl, Leh, Liang, the list went on and on. To these had been added others. The Japanese planes crisscrossed the countryside, shooting at anyone who moved. Farmers, women, even children in the streets were shot down. Francis had been shot in the hand and had lost three fingers. Others were hurt much worse. As news of Gladys's hospital filtered through the hills, more and more injured and homeless, young and old, arrived at Bei Chai Chuang. There was much to do. As Gladys set to work that morning, a Chinese woman entered the cave. She saw Gladys and smiled, "Already, Gladys? You should have slept a little longer at least. You'll wear yourself out."

Gladys looked up at the woman whom the villagers called the "Bible Woman." "Good morning," she said, smiling. "God has given us a beautiful morning to work."

"Yes, I was thinking as I walked over that Francis might like to sit outside today."

"A good idea," Gladys replied. "Less will take him out this morning when he comes to help us."

"Have you heard any news of Tsechow?" the Bible Woman asked.

"The last I heard it was still occupied by the Japanese," Gladys answered. "Are you worried about your family?"

The Bible Woman nodded. "Them and others."

Gladys understood. She, too, had friends at the Tsechow mission. The Davies, missionaries from England, had been friends of hers for a long time. And Mr. Lu was still there.

"God will protect them," she said comfortingly.

"I know," the Bible Woman replied softly. "Perhaps we will hear more soon."

News came in the form of a desperate, ragged muleteer named Hsi Lien. He was one of those muleteers who had stayed at the Inn of the Eight Happinesses. There he had heard the story of Jesus Christ and accepted Him as his Saviour.

Hsi Lien crawled over the rocky trail to Bei Chai Chuang and collapsed at the gate, calling for Ai-weh-deh.

"I'm here, Hsi Lien, I'm here," she kept saying as he was led to a room. "What is wrong?"

"The Japanese came to Chowtsun, my town. They insisted that I carry ammunition for their army."

Gladys looked over his head at the Bible Woman. "And did you?"

"Never! I told them I was a Christian. They tied me to a post and burned my house." Hsi Lien began to weep. "They barred the doors and wouldn't let my wife and children out."

"Oh, Hsi Lien," Gladys knelt beside him. With tears running down her own cheeks, she prayed with the young man she had led to the Lord.

Gladys, the Bible Woman, Hsi Lien, and two strong farmers set off across the mountain to Chowtsun, traveling at night to avoid being seen. In the early light of morning they gathered in Hsi Lien's blackened courtyard. Gladys stood on a heap of stones. The others bowed their heads as she read John 14:1-4.

> Let not your heart be troubled: ye believe in God, believe also in me. In my Father's house are many mansions: if it were not so, I would have told you. I go to prepare a place for you. And if I go and prepare a place for you, I will come again, and receive you unto myself; that where I am, there ye may be also. And whither I go ye know, and the way ye know.

When Gladys returned to Bei Chai Chuang, she took Hsi Lien with her. The rest of that year she divided her time between the hospital, Yangcheng, and the villages where small Christian communities had been established. Well over one hundred children crowded into the small village of Bei Chai Chuang. War orphans had been sent to Gladys by both villagers and soldiers; others had simply come on their own, trusting Ai-weh-deh to take them in.

When the winter snows blocked the mountain passes, Gladys stayed in the village to teach the children. By now she depended on the older children to help with the younger ones. Less was respected by the children and they followed his leadership, although he was younger than some of the newer children. He, helped by Ninepence and Sualan, taught some of the younger ones while Gladys taught Bible to the older children.

When the snow thawed, Gladys received word that the Japanese were marching again. She went back to Yangcheng. The Mandarin had called his people together. They listened to the orders of a Chinese Nationalist commander. "Use the scorched-earth policy," he told them. "Burn your crops. Leave your houses without roofs. Let nothing give shelter to the enemy!"

"How shall we live?" the people wondered. "What shall we eat?"

"We shall take to the hills again," the Mandarin decided. "In the shelter of small hidden valleys we can grow enough grain to survive."

Gladys almost laughed. Her life wouldn't change. She would live at the hidden village of Bei Chai Chuang and leave the inn as it was, its bombed roof open to the sky.

She was surprised when the Mandarin turned

to her. "We have done almost everything the soldiers asked," he said. "Except for one thing. The Pagoda of the Scorpion still stands."

"Can't you destroy it?" Gladys asked, puzzled.

"It is believed that long ago a giant scorpion roamed these mountains, devouring our people. One day while it was sleeping, our people quietly built this pagoda around its head, trapping the scorpion forever. Now they fear that the destruction of the pagoda might free the scorpion."

"Do you believe that?" Gladys asked in amazement.

"No, I do not," the Mandarin answered, smiling. "But that is why I want you and your Christians to destroy the pagoda."

"Gladly," Gladys answered.

"Afterwards we will have a feast to celebrate," the Mandarin said. "It will probably be the last feast in Yangcheng. The crops will also be destroyed."

The next morning a group of Christians broke the stones loose and tumbled the Pagoda of the Scorpion to the ground. That night at the feast Gladys was seated at the right side of the Mandarin. Surprised at being the guest of honor, she listened carefully to the Mandarin's speech.

He spoke simply to the people of Yangcheng, recalling how Ai-weh-deh came to the city. He spoke of the work she had done among them, of the poor, of the convicts, and of the new faith called Christianity that she had brought with her.

"I have talked with Ai-weh-deh many times," he told the townspeople, "about her religion. She has told me about Jesus Christ. I told her about the Perfect Man. Now I know that we will never become perfect except through Jesus Christ."

Turning to Gladys, he said to her, "Ai-weh-deh, I would like to accept your faith. I want to become a Christian!"

My Grace Is Sufficient

11

The war went on. Outside the gates of Bei Chai Chuang the trees put forth the buds of early spring. The heavy snows of winter melted, again making travel through the high mountain passes possible.

"Ai-weh-deh! Ai-weh-deh!" The cry came from the gate. Gladys was needed. This time a convert near Chin Shui had been attacked by bandits. He had sent a messenger to bring Gladys.

"Ninepence," Gladys called to the young girl who appeared around the corner of the farmhouse, chasing two giggling, mud-covered little boys.

"Yes, Mother?" Ninepence caught the boys by the collars of their padded coats and held on tightly. Breathing hard, she hauled the squirming boys over to Gladys.

Gladys frowned at the boys. "Precious Bundle, just look at you! And you, Chang! You're covered with mud! What have you been into?"

"Farmer Lui's pigpen," Ninepence panted. "They let the shoats out, and they are rooting up the tender new shoots of wheat."

She didn't have to say more. The distant shrieks of both man and piglets told Gladys how well, or rather how badly, the recapture was going.

"You, Precious Bundle! You, Chang!" Gladys spoke sharply. "Go catch those shoats! And then go to the hospital. The Bible Woman will see that you are dealt with this afternoon!"

Laughter gone, the two boys looked at Gladys solemnly, and then turned to walk away. "Wait," Gladys said. She held out her arms as the two boys turned around. "I'm going to Chin Shui for a while. You two boys must obey the Bible Woman while I am gone."

Precious Bundle threw his arms around her. "I'm sorry, Mother," he said tearfully. "We won't do it again, and we'll help catch the baby pigs, won't we, Chang?"

Chang nodded, leaning on Gladys's shoulder. Gladys gave them a hug and let them go. They ran off in the direction of the wheat fields.

"May I go with you this time, Mother?" Ninepence asked.

Gladys shook her head. "Not this time, Ninepence. The Bible Woman needs you and Sualan to help with the children, and Less must help in the hospital. Timothy will go with me. Have you seen him?"

"Yes, Mother," Ninepence replied. "He is playing with some of the other boys under the grape arbors. I will get him for you."

Gladys started back up the steps to her room. Then she stopped, ran down, and hurried to the hospital. Less was carefully rolling torn cloth to be used as bandages. Gladys watched him for a minute. Quiet all his life, Less had grown into a serious twelve-year-old, responsible enough to help at tasks usually assigned to the older children. He looked up as Gladys stepped into the cave. "Less," Gladys said softly, trying not to disturb the patients. "I'm leaving for a while. Ninepence knows, and so do some of the others. Help her keep an eye on the younger ones. They are getting too wild lately."

Less smiled. "The warm winds of spring have stirred their spirits," he said. "Yes, I will watch out for them."

"I'll be back as soon as I can," Gladys said. "Good-bye, Less."

"Good-bye, Mother. Don't worry about us. We'll be all right."

Gladys smiled and walked quietly over to a seventeen-year-old girl bending over a cot. "Come, Wan Yu." Gladys motioned her outside. "I am going to Chin Shui. Your family lives some miles from there, don't they?"

Wan Yu nodded.

"Would you like to go with us? We would take you on to visit your mother," Gladys continued.

"Oh, yes, Ai-weh-deh!" Wan Yu replied happily.

Three people left Bei Chai Chuang that afternoon. Gladys carried her medicine, Wan Yu walked beside her, and nine-year-old Timothy ran up the trail ahead of them, hitting the rocks with a stick he had picked up.

Near Chin Shui, they reached the convert's house. Gladys bandaged his wounds, and they stayed with him for almost a week. Then Gladys insisted that they must go on to the town of Chin Shui, and then to Wan Yu's village. After a winter inside the village gates, walking was a pleasure. The newly plowed and planted earth was patch-worked by terraced fields. Timothy darted from

one side of the road to the other discovering treasures—a frog, a grasshopper, or unusual stones unearthed by the farmer's plows. Sometimes Gladys stopped to speak to the men as they worked, one plowing and one pulling the plow.

"Have you seen any Japanese?" Gladys asked. The men shook their heads. "Not yet," they answered, "but no doubt they will be here soon." The men hurried back to their plowing, trying to get as much work in as possible before the planes came again. Gladys, Wan Yu, and Timothy went on.

The first night on the road they were caught in a thunderstorm and had to stop at an inn. Heavy spring rain drummed on the tile roof as the travelers slept. The next morning the roads were slippery with mud. When the roads had dried out, they went on. Timothy amused himself by throwing mudballs at the scrawny bushes alongside the road. They had only gone a few miles before planes began to roar overhead. Throwing themselves flat on the ground, they covered their heads. In the distance they heard the explosion of bombs.

Wan Yu raised her head to look at Gladys. "The Japanese are bombing Chin Shui!"

Gladys nodded grimly. Chin Shui was still a day's journey by walking. If the rain and mud hadn't delayed them they would be in the midst of those falling bombs.

"We must hurry. They will need help after

the bombing," Gladys said. They scrambled to their feet and hurried down the road.

At Chin Shui they found a familiar scene. The villagers hurried about, preparing to flee into the mountains. Foot soldiers attacked, and the villagers fled to the safety of the harsh mountain ranges. When the soldiers left the villages, the villagers crept out of their hiding places and rebuilt their towns. Again and again this was repeated. Gladys understood the villagers' desire to keep small patches of land they could call their own. Early in the war, she had written home, "Do not wish me out of this or in any way seek to get me out, for I will not be got out while this trial is on. These are my people; God has given them to me; and I will live or die with them for Him and His glory."

As the three travelers joined the fleeing villagers, the postmaster saw them. "Ai-weh-deh!" he called frantically. As Gladys reached him, he thrust a large, brown-paper bundle into her hands. "These letters are for you," he said hurriedly. "They were sent on from Yangcheng. My stamps and documents are in there too. Will you keep them for me?"

Gladys agreed quickly, and the postmaster disappeared into the crowded street. Gladys clutched the long-awaited letters from home and hurried to the mission. There they gathered up all the Bibles they could carry, and then joined the mass of people swarming through the village's

West Gate. Three hundred yards down the road from the gate, Gladys, Wan Yu, and Timothy followed the villagers into the swiftly flowing Li river.

The rushing water was chest deep on Gladys. She balanced her precious letters on her head and clutched Timothy with one hand. Wan Yu struggled along behind them, holding the bundles of Bibles high.

On the other side they hurried up the steep slope to the mountains, where Wan Yu's mother lived. Behind them they heard the crack of rifle fire as the Japanese entered the city.

There were no paths up the side of the mountain. They struggled up through terraced fields of millet. All day they climbed upward. Wan Yu's village was almost at the top. Only one village lay beyond it.

In Wan Yu's house lived her mother, her brother, and his wife. A few hours after Gladys, Timothy, and Wan Yu arrived, they were joined by others fleeing the walled city below.

Gladys could not return through Chin Shui to Bei Chai Chuang. Trusting the Bible Woman and the older children to take care of her huge family there, Gladys settled down to work at the village. Once again she started a small hospital and prayed that the Japanese would come no closer.

Almost every day the Japanese would leave Chin Shui and attack the seven villages that lay along the river. At nightfall they returned to Chin Shui and barred the gates. Under cover of the darkness, Gladys and the farmers would creep down and help the wounded.

Five weeks later the Japanese began to raid the villages farther up the mountain. With sinking heart, Gladys knew that it would be only a matter of time before they reached Wan Yu's village.

One afternoon Gladys was tending a sick woman in the room upstairs. She heard Wan Yu's shrill scream, "They're here, they're here!"

Quickly Gladys ran downstairs and across the courtyard to a small hole cut in the courtyard wall. She saw khaki-clad figures moving up the terraced fields. Wan Yu's house was the first in the village. There could be no escape!

"Hide," she shouted to Wan Yu. "I'll try to keep them out!"

Gladys ran to the front gate. "Oh, God," she said, leaning against the gate. "Perhaps if they see a 'foreign devil' they will be so surprised they will forget about the others. I don't know what to do. Please help me!"

Into the fear and confusion of her mind came a verse, "My grace is sufficient for thee: for my strength is made perfect in weakness."

Gladys stood straight and pushed open the heavy doors. She stepped outside, expecting to hear gunfire. Instead she heard Wan Yu's voice calling from the balcony, "Ai-weh-deh, they've turned back! They're going away!"

The Japanese never came back to Wan Yu's village. In late summer they moved back into the larger cities, away from the mountain ranges where they could be trapped by the heavy snow.

Gladys returned to Bei Chai Chuang. Her growing family of refugee children had grown too large for the small mountain village. Leaving the Bible Woman in charge of the hospital, Gladys moved back to Yangcheng, taking the children with her. They wound down the mountainside and through the streets of the city of Yangcheng, greeting old friends as they went. At the Inn of the Eight Happinesses, the children swarmed into the courtyard. It had been almost two years since the children had seen their home. The new children explored the rooms of the inn as the others found old possessions—Precious Bundle's broken toy, a favorite book belonging to Less. Ninepence looked for the old cat, but he was never seen again. The winter settled in again, heaping snow into the courtyard and sending the children inside to the warm k'angs.

It was spring again when Gladys met the Chinese Nationalist leaders. In passing, she mentioned to one of them that she saw Japanese troops in her travels. The soldiers asked her to tell them where the Japanese were.

Surprised, Gladys did so. Hesitant at first, Gladys came to realize that this was another way to help her people. "I would help if this were England," she thought. "I am Chinese now.

This is my country. I'll help them in any way I can."

Sometimes Gladys passed troops on her journeys from one church to another. As time passed, some of the Japanese Christians came to her services, having heard of "the storyteller" from the villagers. Gladys watched and listened. And as she moved across the mountain from village to village, she remembered everything she saw. The reports she gave the Chinese army saved the lives of many villagers.

Remembering what had happened to Hsi Lien's family, Gladys realized that her activities might put the children in danger. Arrangements were made to send half of them away. One hundred of the children left with Mr. Lu for the long trip to Sian.

One night a young Chinese soldier knocked on the door of the mission where Gladys was teaching. "You are in danger," he warned. "The Japanese know that you have been giving us information. They have put a price on your head," he told her. "They are looking for you now."

"Me?" Gladys murmured in shock.

"Here," the soldier handed Gladys a tattered handbill. "Read for yourself."

Holding the small handbill up to the lamplight, she read,

> One hundred dollars reward! One hundred
> dollars reward will be paid by the Japanese
> Army for information leading to the

capture, alive, of any of the three people listed below.

Gladys stared at the three names. The first two were important men of Tsechow. The third line read, "The Small Woman known as Ai-weh-deh."

"Thank you," Gladys whispered to the dark figure in the doorway. "Thank you for warning me."

The soldier nodded and left quietly. Gladys turned the paper over and over in her hands. "I can't leave," she thought. "What about Ninepence, Less, Precious Bundle? What about all my children?" Only half of the children had been sent to safety in Sian. Horrified, she thought of the last hundred children that were still gathered at the Inn of the Eight Happinesses. "I can't leave them."

By morning she realized that she would be no help to anyone if she were captured. "I'll take the children with me," she thought, rolling her belongings into a tight bundle.

As she reached the front gate of the mission she heard pounding. "Open up," called the Japanese. "Open up!"

Gladys turned and ran. Out the back gate she sped. As she raced through the graveyard she heard shouts behind her, then the whine of a bullet as it glanced off a tombstone. Gladys dodged. She bent over and ran from tombstone to tombstone. She dashed for the safety of a deep ditch. But just as she reached the ditch, she was hit by a bullet. Gladys twisted and fell on the brink of the ditch. Her crumpled figure lay still, just short of safety.

Across the Mountains 12

Gladys lay still for a moment. Then she moved carefully. A sharp, burning pain shot across her shoulder blades. "The bullet went right across my shoulders," she thought. "I'm not dying! I'm hardly hit!"

Then, seeing the puffs of dust that the bullets made as they hit the ground around her, she realized that she wasn't safe yet. The soldiers were using her fallen body as target practice!

Gladys tore open the fastenings of her padded coat and wriggled out of it. Her Bible had fallen under her stomach. Using it as a sled, she edged forward. She pushed with her toes, pulled with her hands, inch by inch. Then quickly she tumbled over into the ditch. Above her head she could hear bullets spattering into the discarded coat. Gladys bent over and ran.

When she came to a spot where wheat grew above the ditch, she climbed out. Parting the wheat with her hands, she squirmed into the center of the field. Gladys stayed where she was, knowing that the Japanese would lock themselves in the city at dark. Curling up into a ball, she slept.

When Gladys awoke the sun was high in the sky. She tunneled through the wheat to the edge of the field and lay still, waiting. As soon as the shadows darkened the valley, she slipped out of her hiding place and hurried across the rolling hills to the mountains.

Two days later she arrived at the Inn of the Eight Happinesses. Tired and aching, she stumbled into the courtyard.

"Ai-weh-deh!" The shouts of the children brought Ninepence running.

"Mother!" she cried. "What's wrong?"

"We must leave here, Ninepence." Gladys looked around at the children close to her. "Where is Less? And Liang?"

"Here, Mother." The two boys pushed through the children to reach her side.

"Tonight," Gladys told the younger children, "I want you all to get a good rest. We will take a long, long walk tomorrow!"

Ninepence ran ahead to open the door as Less helped Gladys to the house. Sualan hurried to prepare something for Gladys to eat. As the steaming bowls of boiled wheat strings and vegetables were placed before her, she told her oldest children and the missionary workers why they must leave. "It is no longer safe to stay in Shansi," she said. "The Japanese have placed a price on my head. We must join the other children in Sian. We'll leave at dawn. I must see that everything is packed for the journey."

"No," Ninepence said gently. "You need to rest if you are going to walk that far. Sualan and I will see that everything is ready."

"We will help," the other workers told her, "but we must stay here. There will be other children coming. We'll keep the inn open for them, but you must go before the soldiers come here to arrest you."

Grateful for once to leave the preparations to others, Gladys lay down on the k'ang to sleep. Late that afternoon she awoke, thinking of her friend, the Mandarin. She got up and left the inn quietly. She went down the road to the East Gate and walked slowly down the war-torn street to the Mandarin's yamen. As her footsteps whispered through its empty halls, she thought back to the meetings that had taken place here. All the splendor and ceremony were gone. When she reached the Mandarin's quarters, only one guard stood outside the big doors.

When the guard saw Gladys, he jerked open the door to the Mandarin's rooms and yelled, "It is she!"

Gladys smiled, thinking that in the old days that would have cost him his head. War had changed many customs.

The Mandarin came forward to greet her.

"Ai-weh-deh," he said warmly. "Welcome!"

"It is good to see you, Mandarin," she said. "Perhaps this meeting will be the last we have. I can stay in these mountains no longer. The Japanese have put a price on my head. I am leaving and taking the children with me."

"Where will you go?" her friend asked sadly.

"Over the mountains to Sian. The other children are safe there."

"The Japanese have reached the Yellow River," the Mandarin said. "It lies between here and Sian. You will have to cross enemy territory."

"We will stay away from them as much as possible," Gladys replied. "We will follow paths the Japanese will never find."

"With a hundred children?" the Mandarin asked in amazement.

"With a hundred children," Gladys replied firmly. "Not one can be left behind."

"And how will you feed them?"

"God will provide. Have you not found that this is so?" Gladys asked.

The Mandarin nodded. "However, for this time, you must allow me to be God's agent. Two men will go part of the journey with you, carrying grain. It will take several weeks of travel to reach Sian. You know that?"

"I know. We leave at dawn."

"God be with you, Ai-weh-deh!"

The next morning Gladys awoke early. Darkness hid the bombed corner of the inn and disguised the broken doors, the sagging balcony, and the rubble in the courtyard. "In a moment," Gladys thought sleepily, "Yang will call that breakfast is ready. The crowded k'angs will stir with the awakening muleteers. Listen, even now the mules move impatiently in the courtyard."

"Mother?" a voice interrupted Gladys's thoughts. She blinked as Ninepence stepped inside the room. It was not the six-year-old Ninepence of the old days, but an older Ninepence. Gladys sighed, fully awake now, remembering where she was and why she was here.

The movement below was not mules, but the older children getting ready for the journey. And behind her the bodies stirring on the k'angs were not muleteers, but children.

"Mother?" Ninepence repeated, her glossy hair swinging in the dawning light as she bent over Gladys. "You are awake?"

"Yes, Ninepence," Gladys replied softly. "I was just thinking of the old days."

"When the muleteers filled the inn with their laughter? When not a sound disturbed the stories of Christ?" Ninepence sighed. "It seems so long ago."

Gladys was surprised. To her it seemed like yesterday. Time in the life of a child is like water, she thought. These children will forget the pain and trouble of war. They will return and rebuild their land, just as their parents did so many times.

"How strong are my people," she said aloud, turning to Ninepence. "Pray with me, Ninepence. Pray that their strength will be in the Lord."

Ninepence followed her mother onto the balcony and knelt beside her. Gently their voices rose on the morning air. When the boys heard them, they, too, knelt on the cool gray bricks of the courtyard below and lifted their voices in prayer.

With the coming of dawn, the inn became alive with the sound of children. Racing back and forth across the courtyard, they played with their bedding, chased each other, and shouted with the joy of morning.

When the Mandarin's men reached the inn, Gladys was ready. The twenty oldest girls, between the ages of twelve and fifteen, rounded up the younger children. The seven older boys, ranging from eleven to fifteen, lined them up. Most of the children were between four and eight years old, young and excited. Sighing, Gladys hung a whistle around her neck, knowing that she would need something to call the more adventurous children back from danger. She looked toward the end of the line. Fourteen-year-old Less waved back at her. He would see that every child left the inn. Gladys nodded and walked out the gates of the inn. The children followed her, pushing and shouting happily. Each child carried his own bedding and his own bowl and chopsticks. The long procession wound slowly through the town and out the West Gate. The younger children left the line, running ahead and then back. Finally, Gladys gave up trying to control them and let them run. Several times she blew her whistle to call some of the boys down off tall outcrops of rock. The long line of children moved raggedly along.

At nightfall they reached a mountain village. As the children wound past a Buddhist temple, a tall priest called out to Gladys in amazement, "Where are you going with all these children?"

Gladys looked at him as he stood on the steps with his long yellow robe wound around his body. "To Sian," she replied. "But we are looking for a place to stay tonight."

"Come in," the priest said. "You can sleep in the temple."

So Gladys found herself curled up at the foot of a golden Buddha, surrounded by chattering children. When they quieted down enough to hear other sounds, they realized that they were not alone in the temple.

"Rats!" shrieked Sualan, leaping to her feet. She was followed immediately by the other girls.

Less, Teh, and Liang found wooden branches and attacked the rats. To comfort the younger children, Gladys began to sing softly. Finally all was quiet again, and the younger children drifted off to sleep. The older boys sat up for a while, but the rats didn't return. At last the boys, too, fell asleep.

The next morning they were on their way again. Refreshed, the younger ones ran and played, climbing the rocks over the trail and leaping down again. By afternoon they began to get tired.

"When are we going home?" they asked. "We're tired, and it's time for our lessons."

"We'll have our lesson while we travel," Gladys said, and she began to tell them a story. Those closest to her could hear, but the others could not, so she began to quote verses instead.

"Say them with me, first girls, then boys," she said. "The Lord is my shepherd; I shall not want."

The girls echoed, "The Lord is my shepherd; I shall not want," and the boys roared, "The Lord is my shepherd; I shall not want!" On the verses went until the psalm was finished. Then one of the girls began to sing, "Rock of Ages, cleft for me." The others joined cheerfully.

By nightfall they were still far from any village. The mists of night covered them damply as they sought shelter under the rocky ledges.

The next morning they arose stiffly and began another day. That evening they met a traveler who invited them to stay at his house.

"How long will it take to reach the Yellow River?" Gladys asked.

"Five days by mule on the regular trail," the man replied.

"How long will it take us, Mother?" Less asked.

Gladys thought of the slow progress they were making on the rocky cliffs. "We're going right through the mountains. On foot, too. Probably about twelve days," Gladys replied, cupping her hands about her bowl of hot tea.

She saw the look Ninepence gave one of the other girls. "I know. The food won't last long. We'll have to trust God as we've always done. He's never failed us, Ninepence."

"I know, Mother," was her gentle reply. "He will take care of us."

In the morning the Mandarin's two men had to go back. The traveler with whom they had stayed provided them with a coolie to carry the grain farther. There wasn't much grain left.

Gladys and the children walked on and on. The older boys led, finding the paths. At one of the villages they had found a bucket of whitewash. Liang and Teh used it to write messages on the rocks for the younger ones to follow.

"This is the way. Walk ye in it!" they read, and squealed in delight. Eagerly they rushed ahead to be the first to find the next message. "Fear not, ye little flock!" met with shouts of triumph. Until the whitewash was gone, the line of children moved along faster than usual.

But after two more nights on the mountain, the whitewash was gone, and so was the grain. The coolie, relieved of his burden, also returned home.

Gladys stopped to look around. The mountaintop on which they stood was bleak and bare. In the distance mountain peaks stretched as far as she could see. Mist curled between them as they rose sharply to the sky. Gladys sighed. The trails to the south were flinty and rocky, the villages few and far between.

"I'm thirsty," Francis said quietly. Gladys glanced down at his hand with the missing fingers. Remembering, she searched the sky again, looking for planes, but saw none.

"I'm thirsty," Francis repeated.

"Look for little places in the rock where the mist left water overnight," Gladys said. There would be no water until the next village. After sipping what drops were collected in the rocky crevices, they began walking again.

They came to a rocky slope that looked impassable. "Which way do we go?" Less asked.

"This way." Gladys pointed to the slope. Less stared at her.

"How?"

"We'll have to hold hands and form a chain. Then we'll pass the younger children down one by one."

The older children carried all the bedding now. The younger ones struggled along, no longer running, no longer playing.

Seven nights out they were in a region unknown to Gladys. The girls' faces were sunburned, their lips cracked. The oldest girls, whose feet had been bound before the governor's law, struggled along a few yards at a time. The children's shoes were wearing out, their feet torn and bruised. Gladys's heart was moved with pity. "How can they make it, Lord?" she asked. Prayerfully she began to sing.

> Guide me, O Thou great Jehovah,
> Pilgrim thro' this barren land;
> I am weak but thou art mighty,
> Hold me with thy powerful hand.
> Bread of heaven, Bread of heaven,
> Feed me till I want no more,
> Feed me till I want no more.

Suddenly Teh and Liang came running back down the trail toward them. "Soldiers!" they cried. "Soldiers!"

The Long Journey 13

Around the bend after the boys came a troop of soldiers. Gladys gave a gasp of relief. They were Chinese Nationalists!

Before they could speak, the roar of approaching planes shattered the air. Gladys, the children, and the soldiers flung themselves under every available sheltering rock. They lay still, heads down and covered, but there was no rattle of gunfire. Instead the planes droned on overhead and were gone.

Gladys stood up and blew her whistle. Everyone scrambled up. The soldiers were mixed up with the children. Both were laughing and chattering. The soldiers opened their packs and began to pull out food, handing it to the hungry children. The soldiers produced food that had not been seen in Shansi for years! The children shouted with delight at each offering. That night, the soldiers camped with Gladys and the children. The children sat around small fires, stuffing themselves with food. Even Gladys ate until she was full. When the troops moved on at dawn, the children waved a sad farewell.

With full stomachs, the children began another day of walking. Without any urging, they began to sing.

> Bread of heaven, Bread of heaven,
> Feed me till I want no more,
> Feed me till I want no more.

The sweet food had revived the younger children. A sound sleep, even on the rocky ground, had given them enough rest to make them lively again. They climbed along happily, once again certain that they were on a holiday. But the older children, taking turns carrying the extra rolls of bedding and the youngest children, began to tire quickly. Ninepence and Sualan were limping badly, and some of the older girls could hobble only a few hundred feet before resting. Gladys saw Less stop beside Ninepence and silently take the child she was carrying and place him on his own back.

On the twelfth day they entered the last range of mountains. It had been several days since the soldiers had shared their food. Everyone was tired, even Gladys. Tired of walking. Tired of being hungry.

The voices of the younger children began to echo in her head.

"I'm hungry!"

"I'm tired!"

"Carry me!"

"When will we stop?"

"I'm thirsty!"

They toiled up another slope that seemed to stretch upward to the sky. When they reached the top, Gladys stopped. "Look," she said. "Look!"

Below them lay terraced fields in shades of green and gold. Through the fields wound a yellow coil of water. Ninepence shifted the tired child in her arms. "The Yellow River!" she whispered. The words were repeated by the other children and sounded back down the line. "The Yellow River!"

As the line of tired children wound down toward the yellow water, a hymn of thanksgiving wavered in the mountain air. Then stronger, stronger it sounded until the air trembled with the voices of a hundred children.

> O for a thousand tongues to sing
> My great Redeemer's praise,
> The glories of my God and King,
> The triumphs of His grace!

Slowly the line of singing children wound down into a village. No one moved in the village; no one came to meet them. Gladys held her hand up for quiet. The singing faltered, then stopped. "Hello!" Gladys called. "Hello," echoed the children. Their voices trailed off into the strange silence. Even the air seemed still, without movement. The village was deserted.

Gladys almost cried. Then, remembering that she must be brave for the sake of the children, she said, "Search for food. Perhaps something is left."

The children found only an old man sitting outside his house near the river. "Where is everybody?" Gladys asked.

The old man pointed to the other side of the broad, yellowish water. "There," he said.

"Why didn't you go with them?" Gladys asked.

"I'm not afraid of the Japanese," he scoffed. "I'm old. I'll die in my own home, not in some stranger's house."

Gladys looked across the water but could see no movement on the other side. "Where are the boats? We must get across the river."

"No boats." The old man shook his head. "They took them all. No one comes here any more."

Stunned, Gladys led the children down to the riverbank. The old man was right. Not one boat was on the river. Not one.

For three days they stayed by the riverside. The children rested. Then they played along the riverbank. Troubles forgotten, they ran through the reeds, splashing water and laughing. Soon the little ones were busily building mud playhouses on the riverbank. Precious Bundle and Chang chased frogs, tadpoles, and minnows through the reeds, laughing and shouting as their prizes escaped.

But Gladys was worried. One hundred children couldn't sit on a riverbank and starve. She sent Less, Teh, and Liang back into the village to search for food again. They came back with a few pounds of moldy millet and a small bag of stale bread and shriveled wheat cakes that had been left in the deserted houses. The girls dumped everything into one pot and boiled it. Gladys carefuly rationed scarce spoonfuls into the bowls of the younger children. She and the older children didn't eat. There wasn't enough for everyone.

Gladys watched the river and prayed for God to send a boat. No one came.

The children became restless. They were hungry. "When will the boat come, Ai-weh-deh? When will we cross the river?"

Gladys shook her head. She took out her Bible and gathered the children around her, reading while there was still light. Then they prayed together before the rolls of bedding were stretched out.

At night the moon turned the yellow water to silver. Night birds fluttered, insects chirped, and the children slept.

The third day the children came to her. "Why doesn't God part the water?" they asked.

Gladys looked at them. "I'm not Moses," she answered.

"But God is still God."

"Then help me pray," Gladys whispered, tears running down her cheeks. Together the children knelt on the bank and prayed. They asked God to get them across the Yellow River as He had helped Moses across the Red Sea. When they had finished praying, they began to sing.

> The Lord's my shepherd, I'll not want
> He makes me down to lie
> In pastures green; He leadeth me
> The quiet waters by.

Gladys listened with pleasure as the verses from the Scottish Psalter floated over the water.

That day a patrol boat came. When the men heard the children singing, they stopped. "What are you doing?" the officer asked. "The Japanese planes fly over this river almost every day. They fire into the reeds and sometimes into the water itself. You're lucky that they haven't come this week!"

"Luck didn't have anything to do with it," Gladys said. "God did."

The officer listened to her story as the children were taken over the river, group by group. When the last boatload reached the other shore, the officer shook his head. "May your God be with you," he said. "You will need His help!"

Safe at Last 14

Gladys and the children found a village about two miles down the river. Although many refugees had already passed through the city, the villagers still welcomed the children. The village elder divided them up, sending a few to each house. Gladys wanted to move on as fast as possible to keep the children ahead of the line of advancing Japanese. When the children had eaten their fill and thanked the villagers, Gladys blew her whistle. She led the children out of the village and down the road. They spent that night in an open field.

The next day they walked to the city of Mien Chu. When Gladys asked for help, she was sent to the refugee center. There she and the children were served from steaming hot cauldrons of food in an old temple. The temple, too, was crowded, but there was enough for all to eat. While the children ate, Gladys asked directions to Sian.

"There is a train," someone told her. "It will be crowded with other refugees, but perhaps you can get on."

"But we have no money for tickets," she cried in distress.

"There is no need for tickets," the man said gravely. "Every train is a refugee train. No one has to buy tickets. Just take the children to the station tomorrow."

Gladys blew her whistle and gathered the children together. When they were quiet, she asked them, "Do you know what a train is?"

An excited murmur arose from the children. No, the younger children didn't know, but the older ones had at least heard about the trains at Yutsa, the only station in the Shansi Province. No one had ever seen a train. Gladys did her best to explain what a train was. Watching their faces, she wondered just how much they understood. Somehow she didn't think the mental picture they were forming was anything like the real thing that they would see in the morning.

"Oh, well," she thought, "they'll know what one is soon enough."

Blowing her whistle for silence, she said, "Now, no one is going to be allowed on that train with dirty faces and hands. There is plenty of water here. Make sure you are clean before you come to the platform tomorrow."

The next day Gladys lined the children up on the station platform. She smiled as she inspected the hands and faces. Not one child wanted to be left behind. Their smooth young skin was spotlessly clean, and even their ragged clothes had been brushed as clean as possible.

"Here it comes!" yelled one of the older boys. All eyes stared down the track. In the distance they heard strange clanging and hissing noises. Then a huge machine charged around the bend, looming larger and larger as it approached the platform. Bedding, bundles, and bowls flew in every direction as the children fled. Gladys blew her whistle in vain. At last the older children reappeared. Less, Ninepence, and the others helped dig the children out from every hiding place imaginable. Some were in barrels stored on the platform. Others were underneath boxes, wagons, and every other movable

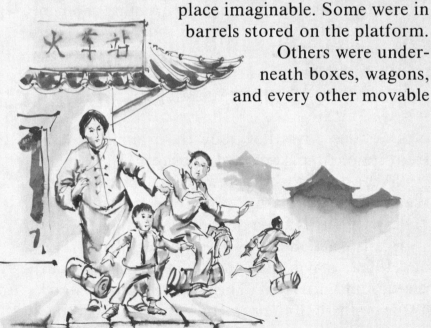

object within a hundred yards of the station. A group of eight-year-old boys had even run all the way back down to the refugee shelter!

At last the embarrassed children were all packed aboard. Because the train had no seats, they sat cross-legged on the floor. Gladys tried to keep them together as much as possible, but it was hopeless. They were mixed in with the other refugees, packed as close as they could get. Some of the boys crowded around one elderly gentleman. The train rattled and swayed across the countryside. As it neared a tunnel, the old gentleman took a candle stub out of his pocket. Carefully he lit the candle.

The boys stared at the bright flame. Gladys never knew which one yielded to temptation. Poof! The flame was blown out. At that moment the train entered the tunnel and was plunged into darkness. Wails and screams came from the terrified children. In a few seconds the annoyed gentlemen had lit his candle again. This time it stayed lit.

For four days they rode the train. Then the train slowed and screeched to a stop.

"A bridge has been blown up. There are no tracks for the train," someone told Gladys. "Everyone walks from now on."

Gladys and her children joined the stream of refugees leaving the train and heading toward the mountain passes. They walked and walked. "At least there is no problem with food this time," thought a weary Gladys. Every village seemed to have heard of them in advance. "You have many mouths to feed," one man told Gladys as he ladled out millet from a huge pot in his farmyard, "but who can resist you!"

On and on they trudged over flinty trails that tore their already worn shoes. When there were no more villages, there was no more food, and they slept on the mountains. Gladys never ceased to marvel at how soundly the little ones slept. They could be moved, even dropped, without awakening.

When the band of refugees neared Tungkwan, Gladys knew that they couldn't walk much farther. Even on bandaged feet, the girls could barely support themselves, much less carry the little ones. The eight- and nine-year-olds were still ahead, but the smaller children had come back to cluster around Gladys. They hung on to her gown, too tired to complain or beg to be carried. The girls stumbled from rock to rock, sitting down every few steps. Even the oldest boys walked listlessly; they, too, were tired and depressed.

For the first time on the trip, Gladys cried. The tears flowed down her face, leaving tracks in the caked dirt. She cried for the destruction of China, for having to leave her work, for bringing the children out into a wilderness where they would surely die. She cried and cried. The children cried with her. Even the eight- and nine-year-olds wandered back, and after staring for a few minutes, burst into tears too. When it was over and done, and the tears wiped away, Gladys felt better.

"Well, that's that," she told the children. "Sometimes a good cry is the best thing you can do. Now don't you think we ought to tell the Lord about it?"

As the children nodded, still wiping tears, Gladys prayed. When she finished, she managed a smile. "Now, you know how to chase the fears away, don't you?"

They nodded again. "Sing," they said.

"Then let's sing," Gladys said. "Let's sing as loud as we can!"

They straggled up and marched down the slopes into Tungkwan, singing at the top of their lungs. The villagers gathered along the streets to watch them in amazement.

Gladys stopped to ask directions again. "Is there another way to reach Sian?" she asked one of the villagers. "My children just can't walk any farther. They are exhausted and so am I."

"There is a train," a villager told her. "But it is a coal train. It runs at night, and even then the Japanese sometimes shoot at it."

"We'll take it," Gladys said firmly. "It's that or nothing."

In the middle of the night Gladys and the older children quietly formed a line reaching from the station to the house where the younger children slept. When the train arrived, the sleeping children were passed from person to person down to the train. Gladys was thankful that the nights on the rocky slopes had taught the children to sleep so soundly. Not one child awoke.

"Tuck them in among the chunks of coal," Gladys whispered. "Then pile the coal up around their heads. Don't let one head show above the coal!"

The children were packed in with the coal. Then older children were assigned to each coal car.

"Shh! Not one sound! Not one cry! If a child wakes up, keep him quiet!"

Gladys walked back along the track and climbed into a coal car. She settled herself gently between Precious Bundle and Chang. Slowly the train began to move. It chugged into the countryside. Gladys dared not look outside for fear the Japanese would see her and begin to shoot. Overhead the moon sailed across a cloudless sky. Sometimes the train passed close to trees and the branches blocked the moonlight for a few minutes. On and on they chugged. Still there was no sound of gunfire. At last the swaying of the coal car rocked Gladys to sleep.

When she opened her eyes, it was daylight. Early morning sun glinted off the chunks of coal. Gladys blinked and looked around. Bright eyes looked back at her from coal-blackened faces. Precious Bundle grinned at her and touched her face, pulling his finger down her cheek.

The children giggled. "Ai-weh-deh is black too."

Gladys felt of her face. It was dirty and grimy. She laughed too. Then cautiously, even though she knew they had to be out of Japanese territory by now, Gladys raised her head and peeked over the edge of the car. Precious Bundle pulled up next to her. Leaning on his elbow, he looked out. The train was rolling through green hills covered with trees. The bright roofs of pagodas curved over pink-blossomed branches.

Gladys heard shouts of delight and laughter behind her. She turned to look back. Black-smeared, smiling faces peered over the edge of each car.

"Look!" called the children of the bleak mountain ranges. "Look!"

Tiny bridges arched over trickling streams, and bells tinkled as the train passed a temple wall. "It's beautiful, Mother," Precious Bundle said. "Are we in Sian?"

"Not yet, but we are close," Gladys replied.

"Then we are safe." Precious Bundle turned to look up at her.

Gladys looked out at the green landscape and then back at Precious Bundle. "Yes, we are safe at last."

An echo came from the car behind Gladys. She listened. Then she heard high, light voices lifted in a song. First one car, then another joined in. The children were singing in Chinese.

Count your blessings,
Name them one by one,
Count your blessings,
See what God has done!

Count your blessings,
Name them one by one,
And it will surprise you
What the Lord has done!

Epilogue

At Sian Gladys and her children found the gates of the great city closed. "Sian can hold no more," a man called to the refugees. "Perhaps in Fufeng you can find help."

Gladys stared at him, too tired and feverish to move. Then the tide of people flowed back from the gate, sweeping some of the children along with them. Taking a deep breath, Gladys blew her whistle and herded her charges back to the station. At Fufeng she found refugee centers and private homes where people agreed to take the children. When the children were settled, Gladys went from one group of refugees to another, telling them about the Christ who died for them. As she walked, the hot sun poured down on her throbbing head. Her bones ached with weariness. In the middle of the afternoon, the sky spun around her, and she fell into the dust of the street.

At the hospital Gladys was delirious with a temperature of 106 degrees. For weeks she struggled with exhaustion, malnutrition, relapsing fever, pneumonia, and typhus. It was months before she was up and about, and years before she fully recovered. To see that she got peace and quiet, the doctors sent her to stay with the Fishers, a missionary couple at Meihsein.

When Gladys was well enough, she went back to see her children. Satisfied that they were being cared for properly, she felt free to continue the Lord's work. She went to Sian, where she found a small room off a courtyard. The courtyard was rented by two Chinese Christians. They had turned one of the rooms into a small chapel and had begun an independent church. At the church, Gladys taught the refugees who streamed into the city. She told stories, sang hymns, led some of the people to Christ, and fed and clothed those in need. As the refugees told others about the church, more and more people flocked to the tiny courtyard.

Although it was over two years after Gladys and her children had reached Sian, the war was still dragging on. Then, in 1943, the Americans landed on one of the islands controlled by Japan. When the Japanese heard, they retreated, and the Chinese countryside was free from troops.

By autumn Gladys was on the move again. She received an invitation to stay with Dr. and Mrs. Hoyte at their home in Lanchow. Gladys accepted, happy to see the blue skies of northwestern China again. The Hoytes' home at the Borden Memorial Hospital topped a barren slope of the Yellow River and faced the walls of Lanchow. The hospital was a busy compound. People from hundreds of miles around came there for medical attention. Gladys found good fellowship, a good home, and lots of work to do. But when she heard of a small group of Christians in a remote mountain village, she packed her belongings and went to help.

When Gladys's work was done there, she went on to Chengtu, where she worked with a Chinese doctor. While in Chengtu, she attended the church of Pastor Christian Chang. When he needed a Bible woman, he asked Gladys if she would accept the position. She agreed and moved into a small room at the back of the church. She cleaned the church, studied, prayed, and taught the women.

At last the war between China and Japan was over, and China enjoyed a few years of peace. Then rumors began to drift out of the north.

The Communists were beginning to move out of their mountain stronghold of Yenan, just the other side of Shansi. The wealthy began to quietly leave the cities, and the consuls asked the missionaries to begin packing. Since Gladys had given up her English citizenship and was a naturalized Chinese, her friends worried about her. If she were arrested, there would be no way they could help her. One of her friends contacted the Orphaned Missions Committee, a society set up to aid missionaries cut off from their home countries. He told them about his "orphaned" missionary and arranged for her to reach England.

Gladys arrived in England in the spring of 1949. Her parents overlooked the small Chinese woman waiting patiently on a wooden bench and had Gladys paged over the loudspeaker. When the brown-skinned woman hurried to meet them, they were startled to realize that she was their daughter.

Gladys was happy to see her family again, but she found herself a stranger in London, as had Mrs. Lawson. The overgrown city was too noisy, too fast, too strange for her to take in. Realizing the difficulty Gladys was facing, Mrs. Aylward set to work trying to make Gladys feel at home. She introduced her to friends and acquaintances. Gladys began to get invitations to speak at churches. The "storyteller" emerged, and Gladys was busy about the Lord's work again, happily telling about Christ and the work in China.

When an article about Gladys appeared in a newspaper, a BBC producer decided to interview Gladys. Alan Burgess was expecting to get a short interview for his program, "The Undefeated." Instead he ended up with a half-hour dramatization of Gladys's life.

Gladys received more invitations to speak. She was content until news from China began to filter back to London. Tales of secret arrests, interrogations, and accusations of brother against brother sent her to her knees in prayer. Finally she realized that she could not return to Communist China. Instead, she turned her attention to the Chinese of London, helping them in every way she could.

The dramatization of her life had been such a success that Alan Burgess was asked to write a book about her life. Gladys agreed to talk to him on the condition that he would come with her to her meetings, as she had no time to spare. He did, and *The Small Woman* was published in 1957.

That year Gladys decided to go back to Nationalist China. She set sail for Hong Kong in April. She was met by old friends and acquaintances and was delighted to see them again. For a while she stayed in Hong Kong, but it was too crowded for her to remain there permanently. She went to Formosa and made the little island of Taiwan her home. Proudly she referred to the island as "Taiwan, Free China."

Some of her friends and even some of the children she had taken on the long journey over the mountains were in Taiwan. Gladys found that she was not only a "mother" but also a "grandmother"! Children flocked to her as always, and soon Gladys was looking for a house to fill with the orphaned children abandoned on her steps and in the streets. The Babies' Home was begun.

By 1959, Gladys was again accepting invitations to speak, this time to tell of the Babies' Home and to seek help for the babies. She spoke in America, then in Canada. In 1963 she was back in London. She took Gordon, a little Chinese toddler, with her. Gladys had taken care of many babies, but Gordon was special. He became her own and went with her everywhere, holding her hand as they walked, and sitting quietly on the platform as she talked.

Her last visit to England was in 1966. She returned to Taiwan to live with Gordon in a small house in the city. Gordon was a schoolboy now. He and Gladys spent many happy hours paddling about in the cove on the seashore. He still attended her meetings and admonished her not to talk too long. Although she enjoyed the speaking tours, Gladys loved the children more. A friend drove her to the Babies' Home two or three times a week. Gladys spent some time there, visiting and playing with the children.

The year of 1970 began like most others, cold and damp. Gladys caught a cold and began to cough. The friend who was staying with her advised her not to attend a night meeting, but Gladys went anyway. When she got home, her cough was worse and she had a fever. The doctor came, told her that she had flu and pleurisy, and gave her some medicine. At the age of 68, Gladys went to be with her Lord.

The news of Gladys Aylward's death was broadcast over BBC. Her funeral service was attended by over a thousand people, and memorial services were held for her in America, Canada, Australia, and England. Her body was not returned to England but was buried on a hillside facing Yangcheng in mainland China, where her ministry began. Although she herself was in heaven with the Father, her body remained with the people she loved. For as Gladys herself had written years before:

> These are my people; God has given them
> to me, and I will live or die with them
> for Him and His glory.

Glossary

Ai-weh-deh |ī wā dər′| —*noun* Chinese name meaning "the virtuous one."

am•mu•ni•tion | ăm′ yə nǐsh′ ən | —*noun* Bullets, explosives, bombs, grenades, or anything else that can be fired from a gun or weapon or can explode and cause damage.

an•cient | ān′ shənt | —*adjective* Very old.

ar•bor | är′ bər | —*noun* A shaded place or garden area closed in by vines growing on lattices.

bar•ri•er | băr′ ē ər | —*noun* Something that holds back or stops movement.

bay•o•net | bā′ ə nět′ | —*noun* A knife attached to the front end of a rifle.

Bei Chai Chuang | bā chī jwäng | —*noun* A small mountain village located in Shansi province near Yangcheng in China.

bom•bard | bǒm bärd′ | —*verb* To attack or bother with words or remarks.

bul•wark | bǔl′ wôrk′ | —*noun* Something, such as a wall, used for protection.

cash | kăsh | —*noun* A Chinese coin.

caul•dron | kôl′ drən | —*noun* A large kettle.

cem•e•ter•y | sěm′ ǐ těr′ ē | —*noun* A graveyard.

Chang | chăng | —*noun* A Chinese name.

Chin Shui | chēn shwē | —*noun* A walled city in the Shansi province of China.

cit•i•zen•ship | sǐt′ ǐ zən shǐp′ | —*noun* The duties and rights of a citizen.

cleft | klěft | —*verb* Divided.

con•vert | kǒn′ vûrt′ | —*noun* One who has been persuaded to adopt a particular religion or belief.

con•sul | kǒn′ səl | —*noun* An official appointed to represent his people in a foreign country.

coo•lie | **kōō′ lē** | —*noun* An unskilled worker in the Orient.

crev•ice | **krĕv′ ĭs** | —*noun* A crack.

crys•tal•lize | **krĭs′ tə līz′** | —*verb* To coat with sugar.

cus•tom | **kŭs′ təm** | —*noun* Something people do that is widely accepted or has become a tradition.

deed | **dēd** | —*noun* A legal document that shows who owns a special piece of property.

di•a•lect | **dī′ ə lĕkt′** | —*noun* A way of speaking a language in different places or parts of a country.

dis•guise | **dĭs gīz′** | —*verb* To hide the appearance of something.

doc•u•ment | **dŏk′ yə mənt** | —*noun* An official paper that can be used to give information or proof of something.

dras•tic | **drăs′ tĭk** | —*adjective* Extreme or severe.

el•der | **ĕl′ dər** | —*adjective* The leader of a village.

fe•do•ra | **fĭ dôr′ ə** | —*noun* A kind of hat made of felt.

for•eign•er | **fôr′ ə nər** | —*noun* A person from another country.

for•tress | **fôr′ trĭs** | —*noun* A fort or other strong place built to resist attacks.

Go•bi Des•ert | **gō′ bĭ dĕz′ ərt** | —*noun* A desert in central Asia.

gorge | **gôrj** | —*noun* A deep, narrow valley with rocky sides.

gul•ly | **gŭl′ ē** | —*noun* A ditch cut into the earth by flowing water.

hoarse | **hôrs** | —*adjective* Low and rough in sound or voice.

hos•tel | **hŏs′ təl** | —*noun* An inexpensive lodging place, especially for youthful travelers.

Hsi Lien | **shē lyĕn** | —*noun* A Chinese name.

i•dle | **īd′ l** | —*adjective* Avoiding work; lazy.

in•ter•pre•ter | **ĭn tûr′ prĭ tər** | —*noun* One who translates spoken messages from one language to another.

i•so•late | **ī′ sə lāt′** | —*verb* To separate from others.

jade | jād | —*noun* A hard green or white stone.

k'ang | kăng | —*noun* A Chinese sleeping platform.

khak•i | kăk′ ē | —*noun* Dull, yellowish brown uniforms worn by soldiers.

ki•mo•no | kĭ mō′ nə | —*noun* A long, loose robe that has wide sleeves and is tied with a wide sash.

Ko•be | kō′ bē | —*noun* A city of southern Japan, located on Osaka Bay.

Leh | lĕh | —*noun* A Chinese name.

Li•ang | lyăng | —*noun* A Chinese name.

lo•tus | lō′ təs | —*noun* A water plant with large, colorful flowers and broad leaves.

Lu | lōō | —*noun* A Chinese name.

Man•da•rin | măn′ də rin | —*noun* A Chinese official.

ma•tron | mā′ trən | —*noun* A woman who is in charge of women or children in an institution such as a school or hospital.

mil•let | mĭl′ ĭt | —*noun* A grass that produces grain that can be used for food.

min•ar•et | mĭn′ ə rĕt′ | —*noun* A slender tower on a mosque.

mis•sion | mĭsh′ ən | —*noun* A place where missionaries do their work.

mor•tal | môr′ tl | —*adjective* Certain to die someday.

mu•le•teer | myōō′ lə tîr′ | —*noun* One who drives a team of mules.

na•tion•al•i•ty | năsh′ ə năl′ ĭ tē | —*noun* The condition of belonging to a particular nation.

nat•ur•a•lize | năch′ ər ə līz′ | —*verb* To declare someone a citizen.

op•er•a | ŏp′ ər ə | —*noun* A musical play that has most of its words sung to music.

out•crop | out′ krŏp′ | —*noun* Rock layers rising out of the ground.

pa·go·da | pə gō′ də | —*noun* A Buddhist tower that has many stories.

par·lour | pär′ lər | —*noun* A room for entertaining visitors.

par·lour maid | pär′ lər mād′ | —*noun* A servant who does light housekeeping.

pass·port | păs′ pôrt′ | —*noun* A document given out by the government of a country, giving permission to travel through the country.

pa·trol | pə trōl′ | —*verb* To go or walk through an area to guard it.

Pe·king | pē kĭng′ | —*noun* Capital city of China, in the northeastern part of China.

per·sim·mon | pər sĭm′ ən | —*noun* An orange-red fruit.

pol·i·cy | pŏl′ ĭ sē | —*noun* A belief or plan of action for doing something.

prin·ci·ple | prĭn′ sə pəl | —*noun* A basic truth or law.

prov·ince | prŏv′ ĭns | —*noun* A big division of a country.

quar·ters | kwôr′ tərz | —*noun* A place to sleep or live.

queue | kyōō | —*noun* A long braid of hair hanging down the back.

ra·tion | răsh′ ən | —*noun* A fixed amount of food for a person.

reef·er (coat) | rē′ fər | —*noun* A heavy, double-breasted jacket.

ref·u·gee | rĕf′ yōō je′ | —*noun* A person who flees from his home to find protection and safety elsewhere.

re·mote | rĭ mōt′ | —*adjective* Far away, not near.

rick·shaw | rĭk′ shô | —*noun* A small, two-wheeled Oriental carriage pulled by one or two persons.

ri·ot | rī′ ət | —*noun* A wild, violent disturbance caused by a large number of people.

scor·pi·on | skôr′ pē ən | —*noun* An animal related to the spiders. The scorpion has a narrow body and a long tail with a stinger that carries poison.

scraw·ny | skrô′ nē | —*adjective* Very thin and bony.

se•dan | sĭ **dăn′** | —*noun* A covered chair designed to be carried on poles by two men.

shil•ling | shĭl′ ĭng | —*noun* A British coin.

shoat | shōt | —*noun* A piglet.

Si•an | sē′ **än′** | —*noun* A large city to the southwest of Shansi province.

spir• it stove | spĭr′ ĭt stōv | —*noun* A small stove that burns alcohol.

Sua•lan | sōō′ ə län′ | —*noun* A Chinese name.

Swan•sea | swän′ sē | —*noun* A town of southern Wales.

ter•race | tĕr′ ĭs | —*noun* A raised bank of earth.

ter•ri•tor•y | tĕr′ ĭ tôr′ ē | —*noun* An area of land; a region.

town cri•er | toun crī′ ər | —*noun* A man who announces news or orders at the town gate.

trans•late | trăns′ lāt′ | —*verb* To change into another language.

Tse•chow | tsē′ **chou′** | —*noun* A walled city located north of Yangcheng in the Shansi province of China.

Tung•kwan | tŏong′ **kwän′** | —*noun* A town located in the mountains between Yangcheng and Sian.

ven•dor | vĕn′ dər | —*noun* One who sells something.

ver•sion | vûr′ zhən | —*noun* Another form of the same thing.

vi•sa | vē′ zə | —*noun* Official permission to travel within a particular foreign country.

vi•sion | vĭzh′ ən | —*noun* The sense of sight; the ability to see.

Vlad•i•vos•tok | vlăd′ ə vŏs′ tŏk | —*noun* A city of extreme southeastern Far Eastern Russia, on the Sea of Japan.

Wan Yu | wän yōō′ | —*noun* A Chinese name.

wares | wârz | —*noun* Things for sale.

white•wash | hwīt′ wŏsh′ | —*noun* A thin liquid used to whiten walls and other surfaces.

Yang | yăng | —*noun* A Chinese name.

Yang•cheng | yăng′ **chĕng′** | —*noun* A walled town in the Shansi province of China.

Yut•sa | yōōt′ sä | —*noun* A town located on a railroad in the northern part of the Shansi province of China.